GAMES AND FUN WITH
PLAYING CARDS

Joseph Leeming

DOVER PUBLICATIONS, INC.
NEW YORK

Published in Canada by General Publishing Company, Ltd.,
30 Lesmill Road, Don Mills, Toronto, Ontario.
Published in the United Kingdom by Constable and Company, Ltd., 10 Orange Street, London WC2H 7EG.

This Dover edition, first published in 1980, is a republication of the work originally published in 1949 by Franklin
Watts, Inc., under the title *Games with Playing Cards Plus
Tricks and Stunts*. The section on contract bridge has been
omitted; the rest of the text is unabridged.

International Standard Book Number: 0-486-23977-2
Library of Congress Catalog Card Number: 79-55672

Manufactured in the United States of America
Dover Publications, Inc.
180 Varick Street
New York, N.Y. 10014

Contents

♠　♡　♣　◇　♠　♡　♣　◇　♠　♡　♣　◇

Contents

12 GAMES FOR LARGE GROUPS

24 STUNTS WITH CARDS

17 MAGIC TRICKS WITH CARDS

Contents   v

25 PUZZLES WITH CARDS

SOLUTIONS TO PUZZLES WITH CARDS

How We Got Our Pack of Cards

WHEN WE PLAY a card game with an ordinary pack of playing cards we seldom think of the long and fascinating history of these pieces of shiny pasteboard.

The very first playing cards were probably made in China or India many thousands of years ago. From these countries they gradually spread throughout the Far East, and then across the Indian Ocean to Arabia and Egypt.

Playing cards were not known in Europe until about the year 1100 A.D., when a number of packs were brought back from the Holy Land by Crusaders. These knights and their retainers had found that the Saracens of Arabia were familiar with playing cards and spent many hours playing different games with them. The cards that they brought back to Europe were all handmade and had beautiful designs carefully painted by hand.

In some of these packs, a variety of materials was used in addition to paper. Some Oriental cards were made of thin painted sheets of wood, ivory, metal, and even of dried leaves. Canvas, leather, and embroidered silk cards are known to have existed, as well as cards of tortoise shell and small tiles.

As soon as the people of Europe learned about these cards, they began to play all kinds of games with them. By degrees they developed the card designs which were the forerunners of our familiar, present-day cards.

In the early packs of cards, each of the suits represented one of the four social classes of the life of the Middle Ages. The nobility were represented by swords, which later became our Spades. The churchmen were represented by cups, which were later turned into Hearts. The merchant class was represented by coins, which later became Diamonds; and the peasants were represented by staves, which later became Clubs. The face cards in these early packs contained pictures of actual kings, queens and princes. In many packs the King of Hearts bore the portrait of Charlemagne, while the Jack of Spades had a picture of one of his famous soldiers, a man named Ogier the Dane.

Later, in France, the King of Clubs represented the Pope; the King of Spades the King of France; the King of Diamonds the King of Spain; and the King of Hearts the King of England. The Queen of Spades at that time represented Joan of Arc.

Some of the early playing cards were round in shape, and some were square. It was many years before cards took the easy-to-handle, oblong shape we know today.

Playing cards were first brought to America by the sailors on Columbus's first voyage to the New World in 1492. They took their cards back to Spain with them, however, and it was not until Cortez conquered Mexico in 1521 that playing cards were really introduced into America. After that the other explorers—and there were many of them—brought more packs of cards to this country and card playing became popular in many camps and settlements established in the New World.

Later on, when America began to manufacture its own playing cards, an effort was made to get rid of the Kings and Queens. A picture of George Washington took the place of the King of Hearts, and the card was called the President of Hearts. John Adams, our second president, replaced the King of Diamonds; and Benjamin Franklin and the Marquis de Lafayette (who had come from France to help us win our freedom) replaced the King of Clubs and the King of Spades. The four Queens became the Goddesses of Love, Wisdom, Fortune, and Harvests; and four fierce-looking Indian chiefs took the places of the Jacks.

But this patriotic pack of cards never became really popular. People were too accustomed to the other designs, and soon went back to them.

Some of the cards have romantic or historical associations that are but little known to most people of today. Do you know, for example, which card is known as "the Curse of Scotland"? This is the Nine of Diamonds, which got its strange name in 1746, when the cruel Duke of Cumberland wrote an order on that card, commanding his troops to show no mercy to the Scottish soldiers captured at the Battle of Culloden.

The Six of Hearts, on the other hand, is known to some people as the card of "loyalty at the risk of death." This is because in 1688 an English soldier, Colonel Richard Grace, used this card to write a refusal to surrender and sent it to William of Orange. Colonel Grace was loyal to King James II of England, and risked being shot or hanged for his refusal to give up. The words that Colonel Grace wrote were, "Tell your master I despise his offer, and that honor and conscience are dearer to a gentleman than all the wealth and titles a prince can bestow."

There are other fascinating things about a pack of cards that few people ever stop to think of. As legend says:

The fifty-two cards in the pack correspond with the fifty-two weeks of the year. The thirteen cards in each suit are the same in number as the thirteen lunar or moon months of each year, and also the thirteen weeks in each quarter of the year. In addition: there are four suits, just as there are four seasons in the year. The twelve face, or court, cards correspond with the twelve calendar months of the year.

It is sometimes said that the total value of the cards in the pack, counting Jacks as 11, Queens as 12, and Kings as 13, is 365, or the number of days in a year. This is almost correct, but not quite. The total value of all the cards is 364.

There is an old calculation, however, which comes out to 365. It goes as follows:

Number of pips (spots) on all plain cards . . 220
Number of pips on all court cards 12
Twelve court cards, counted as 10 each . . 120
Number of cards in each suit 13

*The total equals the number of days in the
year 365*

Card games are played in just about every country in the world today and, to a large extent, games that are very similar are played in different countries. Most of these present-day games are based on old ones that have been played for hundreds of years.

This book contains games that are both old and new, since one of the principal reasons for writing it is to introduce its readers to really good card games, which they may not already know. In selecting these, many people were asked which games they liked the best, and these were included, since experience has shown that they are the most popular.

Readers may find that some games they do already know are presented here with small variations from their own rules. As with many other things, card games have slight changes, or even different names, in different parts of the country. The rules given here seem to be the most widely accepted ones. It is always a good idea before you start playing, however, to be sure that everyone agrees on the rules.

Card Playing Terms and Procedures

MOST PEOPLE know the meaning of the principal terms used in card playing and the general procedure in connection with cutting for the deal, dealing, and so on. A little information on these points is included here chiefly for beginners, but it may also be useful, on occasion, to more experienced players.

Suits. In a standard pack there are 52 cards, divided into four suits of 13 cards each. There are two black suits, Clubs and Spades, and two red suits, Hearts and Diamonds. The cards are named, and run from Ace, Two, Three, etc., up to Jack, Queen and King, in each suit.

Values of the Cards. Depending upon the game being played, the Ace may be either low in value, counting as 1, or it may be the highest card of all, counting more than the King. The value of the King is usually 13. The Queen usually counts 12, and the Jack 11. In some games, however, these cards are counted as 10 each. The other cards usually have the same value as the number of their spots. The King, Queen and Jack are called face cards, court cards, or picture cards.

Tricks. A trick consists of all the cards played in one round of the players. Thus, if there are two players, a trick usually consists of 2 cards. When there are four players, a trick usually consists of 4 cards, one played by each player. In many card games, the object of the game is to win as many tricks as possible.

Following Suit. In many games, one player (usually the player at the left of the dealer) begins the game by putting a card face up on the table. Usually, the other players must then follow suit. This means that they must play cards of the

[5]

same suit as that of the first card played. If it is the Six of Hearts, for example, the other players must play Hearts, if they have any in their hands.

Trumps. In many games, one of the four suits is designated as trumps, such as "Hearts are trumps" or "Spades are trumps." The means by which a particular suit becomes trumps, for a round of play or for an entire game, varies in different games. Where trumps are used in the games described in this book, the method by which they are selected is explained.

The word "trump" came from the word "triumph." Trumps are, accordingly, triumphant, or winning, cards. In playing a game, cards of the suit that is trumps win over cards of the other three non-trump suits, in taking tricks. When a suit has been named as trumps, its lowest-value card, such as a Two, will beat in play the highest-value card, such as an Ace, of any of the three other suits. The non-trump suits are called "plain" suits.

Cutting. A pack of cards is cut by putting it face down on the table and lifting a top section of the pack, usually containing from about one-third to about two-thirds of the cards. The top section is put face down on the table, beside the bottom section. Then the bottom section is picked up and placed on top of the original top section.

Choosing the Dealer. The method of choosing the dealer varies. In most games the players cut the pack or draw cards from the pack. When a cut is used, each player in turn lifts a top section of the pack and looks at its bottom card, showing it also to the other players. This is the card that he cuts. Generally, the player who cuts or draws the highest card is the dealer, although the rules of some games specify that the dealer is the player who cuts the lowest card.

Dealing. The usual custom is for the dealer to deal the first card to the player on his left and to continue to the left in clockwise rotations, that is, the direction in which the hands of a clock move. Every player must receive the same number of cards in every round of the deal in most games. A round of the deal begins with the player at the dealer's left and ends when the dealer gives himself a card. In some games, the entire pack is dealt out, and the players do not always have the same total number of cards. The cards which each player receives are called his *hand* for the game. Sometimes he can add to his hand by drawing more cards from a center pack on the table. When this is the procedure it is indicated in the directions given in this book.

It is customary for players to wait until the deal is completed before touching any of their cards. This permits all players, including the dealer, to see their cards and begin making their plans for play at the same time.

After the first hand has been played, the dealer for the next hand is usually the player at the left of the first dealer. The deal then continues to pass to the left for following hands.

Building Up and Down. In many solitaires and in some other games, the players "build up" or "build down." To build up means to place the card next highest in value on top of a face-up card already on the table. Thus, if there is a Five on the table, you build up by putting on top of it a Six, then a Seven, Eight and Nine, and so on.

To build down, you put the card next lowest in value on a card already on the table.

In some card games, you build up or down in the opposite color, sometimes called the alternate color. That is, you place a black Six on a red Seven, a red Five on the black Six and so on, to build down alternately.

Game. Game can mean other things besides just something you play. Sometimes you are playing over quite a long period of time, and each time the cards are all played on the table and have to be dealt again, that is a game. At other times, there is a score, like 100, that someone has to make before he can win. In that case, 100 is called "game," no matter how many times you have to deal the cards. Then the first person, or pair of partners, to get 100 wins "game."

20 Solitaires

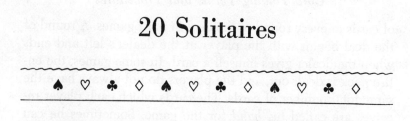

Solitaire games, or Patience games, as they are sometimes called, are wonderful fun at any time. They can be played by one person, and offer a grand way to amuse yourself on trains, on rainy afternoons or evenings, or whenever time is passing slowly. Good solitaires can make the hours fly.

Almost everybody knows how to play Canfield and Klondike, the first two solitaires described in this section; and many people know one or two others. What I hope you will do is to learn four or five of the ones you like the best. Then you will have a way to keep yourself amused and entertained for hours, wherever you are. Solitaires are one of the very best answers to the question, "What shall I do now?"

CANFIELD

This solitaire is said to have been invented by Richard A. Canfield, a famous New York cardplayer. Some people know Canfield as Klondike, and there is another very good solitaire called Klondike, which often goes under the name of Canfield. No one seems to know how this mix-up in names came about. However, by whichever name you call them, you are sure to enjoy both games.

This is how you play Canfield:

1. Shuffle the cards. Count off 13 cards face down into a pile. Turn the pile up and put it on your left. This is your 13 pile, or stock pile.

2. Deal the next, or fourteenth, card face up. Put it out

in the middle of the table, since it is to be a foundation card
on which other cards will be played (Fig. 1). Suppose this
card is a Five. The other 3 Fives, when you come to them,
will then be the other foundation cards. The object of the
game is to play as many cards as possible onto these foundation cards.

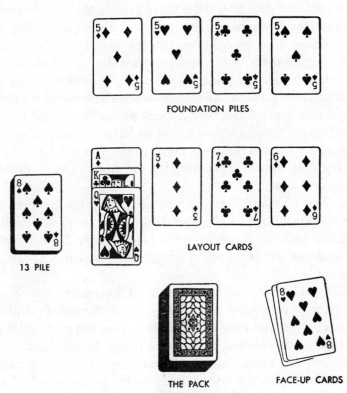

FOUNDATION PILES

LAYOUT CARDS

13 PILE

THE PACK   FACE-UP CARDS

Fig. 1

3. Put the next 4 cards face up in a row between yourself
and the foundation card, as in Fig. 1. We shall call these 4
cards the layout cards.

Now you are ready to play, and this is what you do:

1. Count off 3 cards in a single group, from the top of the
pack remaining in your hand. Put them on the table, all face

up in a pile. In this way, the third card from the top of the pack becomes the top card of the face-up pile. If you can play this card onto a foundation card or onto one of the 4 layout cards, do so, in this way: On the foundation cards, always *build up*, using cards of the same suit as the foundation card. If a foundation card is the Five of Hearts, for example, the next card that goes on it is the Six of Hearts, then, as the game goes on, the Seven of Hearts, and so on. Keep on building up to the King, then go right on with the Ace, Two, Three, and other higher cards until you have played all 13 cards of the suit—if you can. On the 4 layout cards, *build down*, and *alternate* (take turns with) the cards according to color—a red Eight on a black Nine, then a black Seven on the red Eight, a red Six on the black Seven, and so forth. When you get an Ace at the bottom of a column of cards, you can keep right on building down. Put a King on the Ace, a Queen on the King, and so on.

2. *The 13 Pile.* Whenever you can, move the top card of the 13 pile to one of the foundation piles or to one of the columns building down from the layout cards. *Do not build up or down on the 13 pile.* Just get rid of its cards as fast as you can.

3. Continue playing by counting off 3 cards at a time from the pack in your hand and playing the third card if possible. If you play it, you may also be able to play the card under it, and the next cards too, if there are places to put them.

4. You can move onto the foundation piles the top cards from the 13 pile, the layout cards, or the face-up cards dealt out from the pack. Always watch for a chance to do so.

5. While you are playing, you can move cards from one column to another of the layout cards, but they must always build down on a column to which they are moved, and a whole sequence must always be moved at once. A sequence in Canfield is 2 or more cards in a column, each one number lower than the one on which it rests, such as an Eight with a Seven and Six built down on it. If there is a single card in a

column and you move it, it must build *down* on the column to which you move it. For example, you can take a black Eight and put it on a red Nine in another column. But if cards have been built down on the black Eight to form a sequence, you must move them too, along with the Eight. Watch for a chance to do this, since by moving sequences whenever possible, you may make space to put out more cards.

6. If you play or move all the cards in one column, leaving an empty space, you can fill the space *only* with a card from the 13 pile, as long as there are cards in that pile. When the 13 pile is used up, you can fill a space with the top card of the face-up cards on the table.

7. Continue until all the cards in your hand have been dealt face up in a pile on the table. Then turn them face down and deal them off again in groups of 3. Do not shuffle or cut the cards. Keep on until you have either won the game by getting all the cards onto the foundation piles, or can't play any more cards. Then count the cards in the foundation piles to get your score.

Many players follow the rule that cards on top of the four foundation piles may be played back into the four layout columns of cards, whenever they can be used in building a sequence. This is a good variation that adds interest.

Some people play that the cards may be dealt out from the pack in your hand only three times, after which the game ends. Others turn up the cards 1 at a time instead of in groups of 3, and go through the pack only once. There is no strict rule. You can play whichever way you want to.

KLONDIKE

As I mentioned before, this is the solitaire that many people call Canfield. This is the way you play:

1. To arrange the cards for Klondike, shuffle the pack, and then deal the top card of the pack face up on the table. Deal the next 6 cards in a row to the right of it, putting them face

down. Deal the next card face up on the first face-down card.
Deal the next 5 cards face down in a row to the right, partly
covering the 5 other face-down cards. Continue in the same
way until the cards are arranged as in Fig. 2.

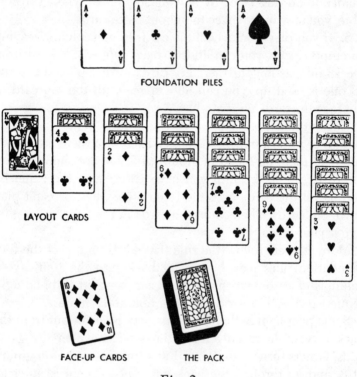

FOUNDATION PILES

LAYOUT CARDS

FACE-UP CARDS   THE PACK

Fig. 2

2. Then deal cards 3 at a time from the pack in your hand,
putting them face up on the table. Thus, on the first deal, the
third card from the top will be face up on top of the dealt
cards.

The original foundation cards in Klondike are the Aces.
Whenever an Ace turns up, you put it out in front of the other
cards. Then you try to build up on the Aces, always adding
cards of the same suit only—the Two of Diamonds on the Ace

of Diamonds, the Two of Clubs on the Ace of Clubs, and so on. The object of the game is to build from Ace to King on the foundation cards of each suit.

3. Cards may be moved from the face-up cards dealt onto the table from the pack in your hand to the columns of layout cards when they build *down* in sequence and are opposite in color to the card on which they are placed. A red Seven goes on a black Eight, and so on.

4. Cards may be moved onto the foundation cards, either from the uppermost of the columns of the layout cards, or from the top of the pile of cards dealt from your hand.

5. Cards and sequences of cards may be moved from one column of the layout cards to another, always building down and being opposite in color. Whole sequences *must* be moved together. You may not move part of a sequence.

6. When you move a card or a sequence of cards from a column and leave the bottom face-down card of the column uncovered, turn this card face up immediately and see if you can play it or move other cards onto it to build down.

7. When you use up an entire column of cards and have an empty space, you can fill the space *only* with a King. After all 4 Kings have filled spaces, however, you can use any face-up card, either from the dealt-out cards or from a column, if the card is not part of a sequence. You can even move a sequence of cards from a column to fill an empty space. There is no rule against it. In fact, it is a good idea, since in this way you may uncover a face-down card which you can use.

8. Continue dealing out your pack 3 at a time, without shuffling. When you have gone through the pack, pick it up and deal it again.

The game ends either when all 52 cards have been played onto the foundation piles or when you can't move any more cards. If you wish, you may limit the number of times you can deal out the pack in your hand. A common rule is that the pack can be dealt out only three times. Others deal the cards one at a time, and go through the pack only once.

ELEVENS

This is a fairly easy solitaire to win. It will probably work out for you four out of every five times you play it.

Shuffle the pack well and then deal out 12 cards, face up, in 3 rows of 4 cards each. If you deal a Jack, a Queen or a King, pick it up from the table and put it on the bottom of the pack. Deal the next card out on the table in its place.

When the 12 cards have been dealt, look for any 2 of them that total 11, such as a Ten and an Ace (which counts as 1 in this game), a Nine and a Two, an Eight and a Three, and so on. When you find 2 such cards, cover each of them with a card dealt face up from the pack in your hand. Whenever you come to a Jack, Queen or King, put it on the bottom of the pack, and deal another card to cover one of the "elevens" cards.

Continue covering pairs of cards that add up to 11 as long as you can. If you can keep this up until you come to the court cards—the Jacks, Queens and Kings—you have put on the bottom of the pack, you win the game. Deal out the 12 court cards, one on top of each pile. This shows that you have won.

PERPETUAL MOTION

Perpetual Motion keeps you busy, moving one card right after the other, until you either win or lose. In this solitaire, you move cards, instead of building them up and down.

Shuffle and deal out all the cards in the pack, *face up,* into 13 piles of 4 cards each. Arrange the piles in 2 rows, with 7 piles in the top row, and 6 piles in the bottom row, as in Fig. 3. The piles represent the cards in order, from Ace to King. The Aces represent 1, the Jacks represent 11, the Queens 12, and the Kings 13.

Look at the top card, face up on pile 1. If it is an Ace, leave it there and go to the second pile. If the top card on pile 1 is not an Ace, put it, *face up*, at the bottom of pile 2. Then put the top card of pile 2, face up, under pile 3; the top card of pile 3, face up, under pile 4, and so on, unless you come to a pile of which the top card has the same value as the pile. In that case, skip over it without touching it. If the top card of pile 8, for example, is an Eight, skip the pile. Put the top card of pile 7 under pile 9, and put its top card in turn face up under pile 10.

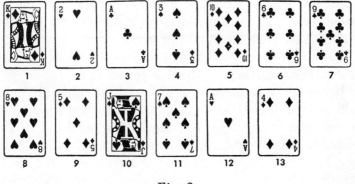

Fig. 3

Move the top card of pile 13 to the bottom of pile 1, unless pile 1 has an Ace on top of it. If this is the case, put the top card of pile 13 under pile 2 or the first pile of which the top card is not of the same value as the pile.

When the top cards of all 13 piles have the same values as the piles, remove these top 13 cards and put them to one side as a completed set or sequence. Begin the next set with the pile where the first set was completed. For example, if the last pile under which you put a card was pile 6, remove the top card of pile 6 and put it under pile 7.

If you can complete and put to one side 3 sets of 13 cards running from the Ace to the King, you win the game. Sometimes you get blocked before you can finish the first set. If this happens, shuffle the cards and start over again.

EVEN UP

Even Up is an easy solitaire. This is how it is played:

Take the Jacks, Queens, and Kings from the pack and put them to one side. Shuffle the remaining cards. Then hold the pack face down in your hand and deal 1 card face up on the table.

Deal a second card. If the total of the second card and the first card is an even number, pick up both cards and put them aside. For example, the first card might be a Five and the second card a Three. Their total would be 8—an even number —so they are picked up and put to one side.

The object of the game is to put aside in pairs all the cards that total even numbers. The Ace counts as 1.

If you deal a card and a second card, and their total is an odd number, leave both cards on the table, face up, with the second card on top of the first. Deal a third card and see if it, added to the second card, the top one, makes an even number. If it does not, put it on top of the second card, deal a fourth card and see if it makes an even number when added to the third card. On each play, you count only 2 cards—the one on top of the pile on the table, and the one just dealt from the hand.

You are allowed to go through the pack only once.

BEEHIVE

This is a good and little-known solitaire. When the cards come off the pack just right, you can win very easily. But many a game gets blocked just when you least expect it.

Shuffle the pack. Then, holding the cards face down, count off 10 cards and put them in a pile face up on the table, with only the top card showing. This is the beehive.

Deal off the next 6 cards, placing them in 2 horizontal rows of 3 cards each. This is the flower garden into which you try to get the bees, or cards in the beehive, as well as all the other cards. Hold the remainder of the pack in your hand, face down.

The object is to combine all the 52 cards in sets of 4 of a kind, such as 4 Twos, 4 Fives, and so on, by grouping them in sets of 4 in the flower garden, and removing each set when it is completed.

With the cards laid out as described (Fig. 4), begin to send the bees to the garden. If the top card of the beehive is the same in value as any card in the garden, place it on that card. Then the next card in the hive, being uncovered, may be used if it has the same value as any card in the garden.

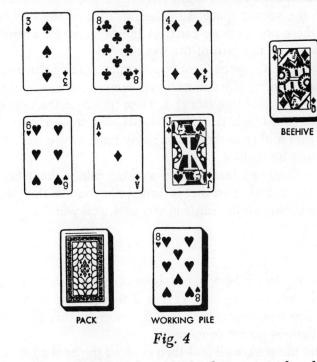

BEEHIVE

PACK   WORKING PILE

Fig. 4

No card is ever placed on the beehive, since the object is to use up all its cards as quickly as possible. Cards are placed only on the 6 garden cards.

If 2 cards in the garden have the same value, place one

on top of the other, and fill the vacant space with the top card of the beehive.

When all the cards of the same value, among the cards on the table, have been combined, deal off 3 cards from the pack in your hand, placing them in a pile face up, with only the top card (the third card from the top of the pack) showing. This will begin a working pile. If the top card has the same value as any card in the garden, place it on the garden card, and use the card it uncovers in the working pile if it, too, has the same value as any in the garden.

When you complete a set of 4 cards of the same value in the garden, such as 4 Threes, remove it, put it to one side, and fill the vacant space with the top card of the beehive. When there are no more cards in the beehive, fill a vacant space with the top card of the working pile.

Go through the pack 3 cards at a time, placing them face up on the working pile and using as many as you can on cards in the garden, building sets of 4. Then turn over the working pile and go through it again, 3 cards at a time. It may be turned over and gone through as many times as you wish, but it must not be shuffled.

If you finally go through the working pile without being able to use a single card that is turned up, you lose the game. If you combine all the cards in sets of 4, you win.

GAPS

Gaps requires a large table, because you have to lay all 52 cards out, one by one. This is a tight fit for most card tables. You can, if you wish, lay the cards out on the floor, where there is plenty of room.

Shuffle the pack well and then deal all the cards, face up, one at a time, in 4 horizontal rows of 13 cards each. Pick up the 4 Aces and put them to one side, and there will be 4 gaps or empty spaces in the layout. The object of the game is to move cards, filling the gaps, so that the Twos will all be in the first spaces at the left end of the rows, and the rows will all be built up in sequence and in the same suit from the Twos to the Kings. One row will be all Hearts, for example, another one will be all Spades, and so on. And the cards in each row are to run in order from left to right, starting with the Two and ending with the King.

When moving cards to fill gaps, you must always build up, putting a card of the next higher value, and of the same suit, to the right of a card already in position. Move the Seven of Clubs to the right of the Six of Clubs, for example; but never move the Six of Clubs (a card of lower value) to the left of the Seven of Clubs. And no card may be put in a gap to the right of a King.

Whenever the first space at the left of a row becomes vacant, it is to be filled with a Two.

Move all the cards you can and then, as a rule, you will find that you are blocked, and cannot move any more. When you get blocked, pick up all the cards that do not form part of a sequence beginning with a Two that is properly placed at the left of a row. Shuffle the cards and deal them out again. Leave one gap after each of the sequences that remains on the table. If there is a row with no sequence beginning with a Two, leave the first space open for a Two.

Strict players allow themselves only one extra deal. But most people allow themselves 3 extra deals and I have found it more fun to play Gaps that way.

ROLL CALL or TALKATIVE

Roll Call is a game in which you have to talk as well as deal out cards. It is also known as Talkative. This is how you play:

Shuffle the cards. Hold the pack in your hand and deal the cards onto the table, one at a time, into a pile, face up. As you deal, count out loud "Ace, Two, Three, Four," and so on up to "Ten, Jack, Queen, King." Whenever a card dealt has the same value as your count, it answers the roll call. You put that card to one side. For example, suppose you count "Ace, Two, Three, Four, Five" and as you say "Five," you deal a Five. You put the Five to one side.

When you have dealt all the cards, pick up the ones that didn't answer the roll call, and deal them again, counting as you do so. Start counting, with the top card, from where you just left off. If the last card dealt was counted 6, call the top card dealt right after it 7.

The object of the game is to get all the cards to answer to their names, and so move all of them from the pack to one side. Some players deal the pack 3 times and then add up the cards removed to get their score. Others continue dealing and try to get all the cards to answer the roll call, going through the pack as few times as possible.

IDLE YEAR

Idle Year is a good name for this solitaire. It is easy to play and you can take all the time you want. The moves are simple and interesting.

Use a full pack, shuffle the cards, and start by dealing them, one at a time, in a row. Watch out for any 2 cards that are of the same suit, such as 2 Hearts, or 2 cards that are of the same value, such as 2 Sevens.

If 2 cards of the same suit or the same value are dealt next to each other, move the second or right-hand one onto the first. For example, if you deal a Three of Hearts and then a Five of Hearts, put the Five on top of the Three. Or if you deal a Ten and then another Ten right beside it, put the second Ten on the first.

Furthermore, if 2 cards of the same suit or of the same value have 2 cards between them, move the second card of the same suit or value to the left, over the 2 in-between cards, and put it on the first.

Watch for opportunities to make 2 or more moves in a row. You might, for example, move a Ten of Hearts onto a Five of Hearts to its left. There might then be another Ten just beyond the 2 cards, to the left of the Ten of Hearts. You could then move the Ten of Hearts and Five of Hearts onto the other Ten.

If a card to be moved already has other cards beneath it, you move the whole pile.

Sometimes you have a choice of putting a card on the card directly to its left or of jumping it to the left over 2 intervening cards. There is no way, in this game, to know which is the better move. You must make a choice and then stick to it.

The object of the game is to move all the cards in the pack onto the first card dealt.

ROUND THE CLOCK

This is an old favorite solitaire with many people. Luck counts a great deal, for the way the cards fall when you deal them determines how close you can come to winning. There is a good deal of fun, and even excitement, however, in trying to work the game out to a successful conclusion.

After shuffling the cards, start by dealing in a circle 12 piles of 4 cards each, all face down, and another pile of 4 cards face down in the center of the circle (Fig. 5). The 12 piles represent the figures on the face of a clock, and they also represent the numbers of the cards from the Ace (1), Two, Three up to the Jack (11) and the Queen (12). The 4 cards in the center form the King pile.

Now try to get all the cards in their correct places, face up, before the King pile is completed—the 4 Aces in pile 1, the 4 Twos in pile 2, the 4 Threes at three o'clock, and so on. Start with pile 1 (the Ace pile). Turn over the top card and put it, face up, at the bottom of its correct pile. If it is a Six, for example, put it face up beneath pile 6. Then turn over the top card of pile 6 and put it beneath its correct pile. If it is a Ten, put it beneath pile 10, and so on. Whenever you turn up a King, it goes face up beneath the center pile.

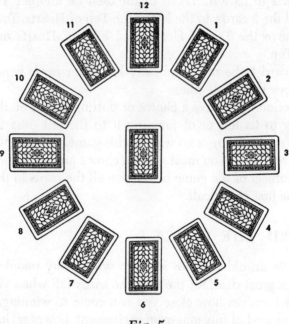

Fig. 5

If you succeed in winning, you will have all the cards in their correct positions, from the 4 Aces at one o'clock to the 4 Queens at twelve o'clock. But if the 4 Kings are turned up before you complete the other piles, the game comes to an end right then and there.

PIRATE GOLD

This is one of the easiest of all solitaires to play—and to win; so if you want to while away some time and have the fun of winning, play a few games and get some of the Pirate Gold.

To start the game, shuffle the cards and deal 5 of them onto the table, face up in a row. Beneath them on the table deal another row of 5 face-up cards, as in Fig. 6.

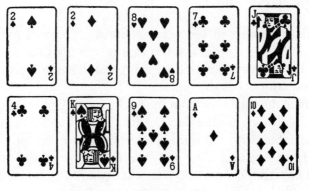

Fig. 6

These cards are called the "pirate's goldpieces." The object of the game is to put other cards on top of them to make piles of gold pieces.

This is how you play:

Look at the 10 cards on the table and see if any 2 of them have the same value and make a pair, such as 2 Fours, 2 Sevens, or 2 Queens.

If there is a pair of 2 like cards, cover each of the 2 cards with a card dealt face up from the pack in your hand. If there is more than 1 pair, cover all the pairs.

The new cards you have added will usually make some new pairs. Cover these by dealing cards from the pack. Then keep on covering pairs and see if you can deal out all the cards in the pack.

If you succeed in doing this, you win the game. But if you get "stuck" by reaching a point when there are no pairs on the table to cover, you lose that game.

It sometimes happens, though not very often, that there are no pairs among the first 10 cards you put on the table. When this occurs, pick up the cards, shuffle them, and deal out 10 new cards.

LAZY BOY

This is another of the easier solitaires. You will probably be able to win it several times in a row every time you play it. But you have to watch the cards carefully as you turn them up, and not get caught napping.

Shuffle the cards and hold the pack in your hand face down. Start by dealing off the 3 top cards and putting them face up on the table, with the third card from the top on top. If this card is an Ace or a King, put it in the center of the table to build on. All the Aces and Kings are put in the center of the table side by side as you come to them in going through the pack.

On the Aces you build up to the Sevens of the same suit, always playing cards of that suit. For example, on the Ace of Hearts, you put the Two, Three, Four, Five, Six and Seven of Hearts. On the Kings you build down to the Eights of the same suit. On the King of Spades, for example, you would put the Queen, Jack, Ten, Nine and Eight of Spades.

Suppose that the first card you turn up (the third card from the top of the pack) is an Ace or a King. Put it in the center of the table. Then suppose that the card beneath it is a Two or a Queen and can be played. You play it also right away, and the card beneath it, if it too can be played.

After you have done all you can with the first 3 cards, you deal off 3 more, putting them face up on top of the others. Play the top card if you can, and any cards beneath it. Then deal off 3 more cards and place them face up on the pile.

Go right through the pack in this way, dealing 3 cards at a time, putting all the Aces and Kings in the center of the table, and building up on the Aces and down on the Kings.

When you have gone through the pack once, turn it over, and without shuffling the cards, go through it again, and play every face-up card you can.

Continue turning the cards over, after each time you go through them, and try to play out all the cards onto the center piles. If you can do this, you win the game. If you cannot complete the building up and down on the center piles, you lose the game.

AULD LANG SYNE

Auld Lang Syne is an old favorite, and it is one of the easiest of the solitaires.

Start by shuffling the cards and putting the 4 Aces on the table in a row. Then deal the first 4 cards on top of the pack in a row beneath them, as in Fig. 7.

Fig. 7

The object of the game is to build up on the 4 Aces, according to suit. All the Hearts go on the Ace of Hearts, all the Spades on the Ace of Spades, and so on.

If there are any Twos in the first 4 cards you put on the table, you can play them on the Aces right away.

If there are no Twos, deal 4 more cards on top of the first 4. Play some of these and some of those under them, if possible.

Keep on dealing in this way until you have gone through the pack. Then pick up the 4 piles for another deal, putting the right-hand pile on top of the one to its left. Put these 2 piles on the one to the left, and the 3 piles on the left-hand pile. Then, according to the general rule, you can go through the pack two times more—or three times in all.

By that time you should have a lot of cards built up on the Aces, or you may even have won the game, for Auld Lang Syne gives you a good chance to win.

GRANDFATHER'S CLOCK

Grandfather's Clock has been a favorite for many years.

You start by putting face up on the table 12 cards—a Two, Three, Four, Five, Six, Seven, Eight, Nine, Ten, Jack, Queen and King. These are arranged in the form of a clock dial but with the Two in the position of the 5 o'clock hand, as in Fig. 8.

The first card—the Two—may be of any suit, but it must be followed by 3 cards of 3 other suits. Look at Fig. 8 and you will see that the Two of Hearts is followed (going clockwise) by the Three of Clubs, the Four of Diamonds and the Five of Spades. The order of the suits that you use for the first 4 cards must be used with each of the other two 4-card sequences.

When you have made the clock dial, deal out the remaining 40 cards of the pack face up into 8 piles of 5 cards each. Put these in front of you below the clock. All the cards in the piles are face up.

The object of the game is to move cards from the 8 piles at the bottom onto the cards in the circle to make the circle represent the numbers on a clock dial. You have to build up the piles in the circle by adding cards of the same suit. Thus, only the Three of Hearts can go on the Two of Hearts. Then the Four of Hearts goes on the Three, and so on. On the Ten, Jack, Queen and King, you build up to the Ace (1), then the Two, Three and Four.

If you are able to play all the cards, the top cards of the piles in the circle will represent the numbers of a clock dial and will all be in the same places as on a clock.

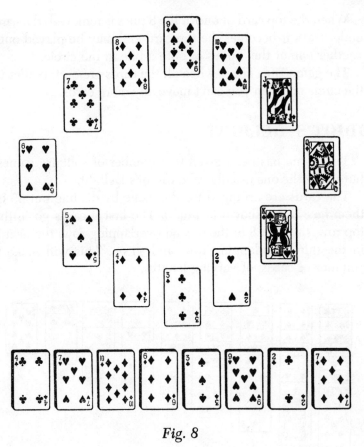

Fig. 8

Here are the simple rules you must follow:

The top cards of the eight piles are played onto the piles in the circle, building up in numerical sequence and suit. This has already been explained in describing the object of the game.

The top cards of the 8 piles may be built down on each other, without regard to color. Thus, you can put either a red or a black Six on a black Seven, a red or a black Two on a red Three, and so on. The colors do not have to alternate. Just let each card be one lower in value than the card you put it on.

When the top card of one of the 8 piles is removed, the card underneath it becomes the top card and may be played onto another one of the 8 piles or onto a pile in the circle.

The game ends either when all the cards are on the piles in the circle or when you can't move any more cards.

IDIOT'S DELIGHT

This name has been given to a number of solitaire games, but this is the one usually called Idiot's Delight.

The cards are arranged for the game by dealing out 45 of them face up as shown in Fig. 9. The first 9 cards go in the top row, the next 8 in the second overlapping row, the next 7 in the third overlapping row, and so on. This will make 9 columns of cards, of varying lengths.

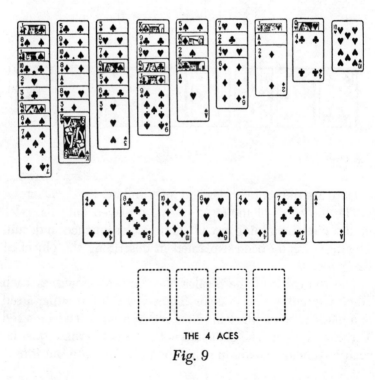

THE 4 ACES

Fig. 9

You will have 7 cards left, and these are laid out face up in a row, below the other cards.

As you play, you will put the 4 Aces below these 7 cards, and will build up on them. The 4 Aces are the bottom cards of the foundation piles. Be sure, therefore, to leave enough room on the table for these piles, which are indicated in Fig. 9 by the 4 cards with dotted outlines.

The object of the game is to build up as many cards as possible on top of the 4 Aces. All the cards in each of these foundation piles must be of the same suit.

The rules of Idiot's Delight are as follows:

Uncovered cards in the 9 columns may be played on each other. In these columns, build down and alternate the colors of the cards, putting a red Three on a black Four, a black Ten on a red Jack, and so on. *You may move only one card at any one time. You are not allowed to move sequences.*

Whenever you uncover an Ace, by moving another card from on top of it, put it below the 7 cards, so that you can start building up on it.

Build up on the Aces in sequence and by suit. That is, put the Two of Clubs on the Ace of Clubs, the Two of Hearts on the Ace of Hearts, and so on up to the King.

Uncovered cards in the columns may be moved onto a foundation pile.

Any of the 7 cards below the columns may be moved to a foundation pile; played on a card in one of the columns, building down and alternating colors; or used to fill an empty space among the columns.

Empty spaces in the 9 columns may be filled by any un-covered card. You do not have to use a King, for example, as in some other solitaires.

You are not allowed to build on the 7 cards, and you are not allowed to fill the spaces made by removing these cards.

The game ends when you have won by putting all the cards on the 4 foundation piles or when no more cards can be moved.

STREETS AND ALLEYS

Streets and Alleys is a fairly widely-known solitaire, which should be even more popular. It is played on the same principle as most other solitaires, but some people like it better because you can build cards on each other regardless of their suits.

After shuffling, the cards are dealt face up onto the table as shown in Fig. 10. There are 4 horizontal rows of 7 cards each on the left, and 4 horizontal rows of 6 cards each on the right. The Main Street runs up the center, and the alleys run off to the right and left between the rows of cards.

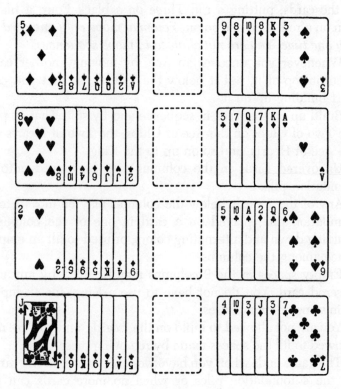

Fig. 10

The 4 Aces are to be placed in the Main Street as soon as you can uncover them, and their final positions are shown by the cards with the dotted outlines (Fig. 10).

The object of the game is to get the Aces out into the Main Street and then to build up on them the remaining cards of their suits—or as many of the remaining cards as possible. Build up by suits—the Two, Three, Four of Hearts and the remaining Hearts on the Ace of Hearts, and the same for the three other suits.

The rules of Streets and Alleys are as follows:

You may move only the outside cards, on the ends of the rows away from the Main Street.

You may move only one card at a time and it must build *down* on another outside end card. Cards can be put beside other cards regardless of color or suit. The only thing that counts is the number or value of the cards. Thus, in Fig. 10, you can move the Seven of Clubs over to the Eight of Hearts. Then you can move the Six of Spades to the Seven of Clubs, following by moving the Five of Diamonds to the Six of Spades. Next you can move the Two of Hearts over to the Three of Spades.

You may not move sequences—only single cards.

When you move an end card, the card next to it becomes an end card and can be played.

When you move away all the cards in any row and leave a space, you may fill the space with any end card you wish to move.

Whenever an Ace becomes an end card, move it into the Main Street and build up on it with cards of the same suit, when they become end cards.

You win the game when you get all the cards out and onto the 4 piles in the Main Street. Sometimes you get "stuck" before that point and cannot move any more cards.

ROYAL MARRIAGE

Here is a first-rate solitaire in which you don't build down or up, as in most others. It works on an entirely different plan, and one that makes you keep your eyes open, watching the cards.

Start by shuffling the pack of cards, and then putting the King of Hearts on the bottom and the Queen of Hearts on the top. The object of the game is to bring these two widely-separated monarchs together at the very end.

Put the Queen of Hearts on the table face up, and deal the 4 next cards in a row face up to her right, as in Fig. 11.

Fig. 11

Now see if you can discard any card or cards by the following procedure: If there are 2 cards of the same suit in the row, but separated by either 1 or 2 cards, pick up the "in-between" card or cards and discard them—not to be used any more. Then move the card on the right over beside the card of the same suit to the left.

Look at Fig. 11 to see how this works. You discard the Five of Spades, which separates 2 cards of the same suit—Hearts. Then you discard the Two of Clubs, which separates 2 cards of the same suit, the Queen of Hearts and the Four of Hearts. Then you move the Four of Hearts and Two of Hearts over to the left, and have Fig. 11-A. Here again the Queen of Hearts and Two of Hearts are separated by a card. This card happens to be of the same suit—the Four of Hearts —but out it goes. You discard it and have the Queen and the Two of Hearts left. Move the Two to the left so that it is be-

Fig. 11-A

side the Queen. Fig. 11 shows cards of the same suit separated by only 1 other card. But if 2 other cards are side by side between 2 cards of the same suit, you may discard both of the "in-between" cards.

Follow the same procedure when 2 cards of the same *value* appear in the row of 4 cards to the right of the Queen. If these cards are separated by 1 or 2 other cards, discard the card or cards between them, and move the card at the right over to the left.

After doing what you can with the first 4 cards dealt out, deal out 4 more cards, placing them in the same positions as the first 4 cards. Some of these will cover cards already on the table—left over from the first deal.

After the second deal, you will probably have one or more *piles* of cards, owing to the fact that you have dealt cards on top of other cards. These piles are discarded just as though each were a single card, when the top card of the pile is one that is to be discarded. There is sometimes a choice of two plays, but in this game there is no way of knowing which will be the best, since your chances of winning depend upon what succeeding cards are dealt out.

Continue dealing out 4 cards at a time until you come to the bottom of the pack. Then, if you are lucky, you may be able to bring the Queen and King together.

HIDDEN CARDS

This is quite a hard solitaire to win. You can, however, figure your score for each game and so, even though you do not win, can count each game as a good one or an unlucky one. The score is the total number of piles of 4 cards that you succeed in turning face up, counting each pile as 1.

Shuffle the pack and deal it, 1 card at a time, face down, into 12 piles of 4 cards each, making 3 horizontal rows, each containing 4 piles. The remaining 4 cards are put in a 13 pile below the other cards, also face down, to be drawn from when needed (Fig. 12).

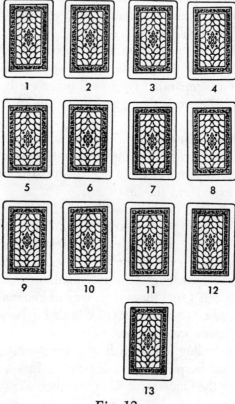

Fig. 12

The object of the game is to move the cards, as described below, so that all the Aces are in the first pile, the Twos in the second pile, and so on.

In this game, the Aces count as 1, the Jacks as 11, the Queens as 12, and all the other cards according to the number of their spots. The Kings are discarded as they appear during the playing.

Start by turning over the top card of the 13 pile, and playing it, face up, under the pile that corresponds to its value. For example, if it is a Nine, place it under the pile numbered 9 in the illustration. Then turn up the top card of the 9 pile and place it, face up, under the pile that corresponds to its value. Keep repeating this process until a King appears. Discard the King and start over again with the next card from the 13 pile.

If the 13 pile is used up, or if the 4 Kings appear before all the cards in all the piles are turned face up, the game is lost.

FIFTEENS

In Fifteens the object is to combine 2 or more cards *of the same suit* whose values total 15 and to discard them; and to keep on making as many as possible "fifteens" in this way. If you can combine and discard all 52 cards, you win the game.

Shuffle and deal out 16 cards in 4 rows of 4 cards each face up, as in Fig. 13. Keep the rest of the pack to deal from as you have spaces to fill.

There are only two things you have to remember. These are:

1. You may combine any 2 or more cards (even 3 or 4 or 5 cards) to make "fifteens." But these cards must be of the *same suit.*

2. In addition, if a Ten, Jack, Queen and King of the *same suit* are on the table at any one time, you can pick up all 4 of them and discard them. This does not happen very often and at other times the Tens, Jacks, Queens and Kings are combined with other cards. The Aces count 1, the Jacks count 11, the Queens 12, and the Kings 13.

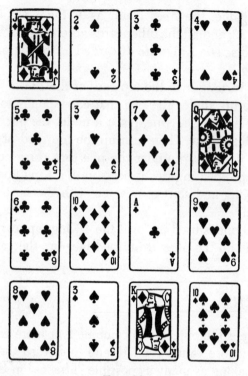

Fig. 13

Now, let's look at Fig. 13 and see what can be done. First you can combine the Three, Four and Eight of Hearts to make 15, and put them to one side.

Next, you can pick up the Ten, Jack, Queen and King of Diamonds, according to Rule 2, and can put them out of the game.

You then have 7 empty spaces. Fill them with cards dealt from the pack in your hand, and see if you can make any more "Fifteens."

The game continues until you win it by combining and discarding all the cards, or until you get stuck and can't make any more combinations.

TEN OF CLUBS

This is a famous and exciting solitaire, in which your success is governed entirely by chance. The game ends when you turn up the Ten of Clubs, and it may be the first card— or the last.

The game is played with 20 cards only. These are the Ten, Jack, Queen, King and Ace of each suit.

Remove these cards from the pack, shuffle them well, and lay them out face down as shown in Fig. 14. The first 3 rows contain 5 cards each, and the bottom row contains 4 cards. The last card is kept in your hand.

Fig. 14

Start by looking at the card in your hand. Suppose it is the
Ten of Diamonds. Place it where the Ten of Diamonds is
meant to go, according to the following arrangement of the
cards:

> *Top Row*   —Ace, King, Queen, Jack, Ten of
>   Spades
> *2nd Row*   —Ace, King, Queen, Jack, Ten of
>   Hearts
> *3rd Row*   —Ace, King, Queen, Jack, Ten of
>   Diamonds
> *Bottom Row*—Ace, King, Queen, Jack, Ten of
>   Clubs

Put the Ten of Diamonds at the right end of the third row
face up. Then turn face up the card that was there in the
first place. Suppose it to be the Queen of Spades. Put it face
up third from the left in the top row, and turn up the card
that it displaced.

Keep on moving the cards in this way until you turn up the
Ten of Clubs. That ends the game right there and then. But
you get credit for all the cards you have turned face up, and
so have either a good game or a bad one.

You can have a lot of fun playing Ten of Clubs with a
friend. Each player has his own pack of cards, and each keeps
track of the number of cards he is able to turn face up. You
can play either five or ten games, and the one who turns up
the greatest number of cards is the winner. You might even
score the game by allowing each player 1 point for each card
he has turned up.

12 Games for Two Players

♠ ♡ ♣ ◇ ♠ ♡ ♣ ◇ ♠ ♡ ♣ ◇

How many times there are when a card game for two players comes in handy to pass the time in an interesting way. I have heard it said that one thing America needs is more two-hand card games, and I think there may be a lot of truth in that comment. Americans love to play games, but when there are only two people, they are often likely to know only Rummy and Gin Rummy, and are at a loss to find another good two-hand game.

So, the idea of this section is to introduce you to the best of the other easy-to-play card games for two. There are some mighty good ones, as you will find by trying out a few of them.

Most of the games in this section are particularly suited for two players and are best known as two-hand games. But nearly all of them can be played by larger numbers. Where this is possible, it is indicated in the description of the game.

RUMMY

Rummy is one of the most widely known of all card games played in America, and has been a favorite for many years. It is a first-rate game for two players, and can also be played, using one pack of cards, by any larger number of people up to six.

The object of the game is to lay down cards by combining them into sets of 3 or 4 cards of the same value, such as 3 or 4 Tens, 3 or 4 Eights, and so on; or into sequences of 3 or more cards of the same suit, such as Ace, Two and Three of

Hearts. The first person to lay down all his cards is the winner.

You should cut the cards to see who deals. The player who cuts the lowest card is the dealer. In Rummy, the Ace is always counted as the lowest card. It counts as 1.

If two people are playing, the dealer gives each one 10 cards. He deals the cards one at a time, first giving one to his opponent, then one to himself, then one to his opponent, and so on.

When the cards have been dealt, the dealer puts the rest of the pack in the center of the table, face down. He then turns the top card face up and puts it on the table beside the pack, which we will call the center pile (Fig. 15).

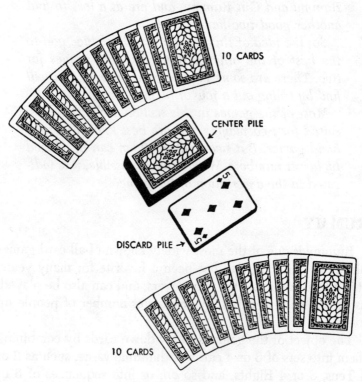

Fig. 15

When two people are playing, the dealer's opponent has the first chance to play. He has two choices. He can either take the face-up card beside the center pile, or he can take the top face-down card of the center pile. He will take the face-up card if it will complete a set or a sequence or if he thinks it will help him to build a set or a sequence. If he thinks the face-up card will be of no use to him at all, he takes the card on top of the center pile, hoping that it will be a good one for him.

Very often, he will have a set or a sequence already made for him in the cards that are dealt to him. He puts these cards together side by side right away. He has to build up other sets and sequences, however, by drawing cards from the center of the table.

After drawing a card, he can lay down any sets or sequences that he has. But—and it is an important but—it is best not to lay down sets and sequences too soon. This is because the other player can add cards to them, and thus get rid of some of his cards.

For example, if you lay down 3 Kings, and the other player has the fourth King, he can add it to your cards when his turn comes, and thus get rid of it. Or, if you lay down a sequence such as the Three, Four, and Five of Clubs, the other player can add either or both the Two and Six of Clubs, to continue the sequence.

This rule works in your favor, too, for if your opponent lays down some of his sets or sequences, you can add cards to them when your turn comes, if you have the right cards in your hand. Both players can also add cards to the sets and sequences they have laid down themselves.

After drawing a card, and laying down cards if he wishes, the player has to discard one from his hand. He therefore looks over his hand and decides which card he wants the least. He discards this one by putting it face up on the face-up card beside the center pile. The face-up cards are called the discard pile.

The dealer in a two-hand game (or the next person to play in a larger game) then goes through the same process. He draws a card, taking either a face-up card or the top card of the center pile, looks over his hand carefully, lays down cards if he wishes, and then discards a card.

Whenever a player feels that the time is right, he can lay down any sets or sequences he has succeeded in making, if it is his turn. He must always lay down cards like these *after* he has drawn a card from the center, but *before* he discards a card from his hand.

The same rule applies to adding cards to sets and sequences that have been put face up on the table. Players add cards only *after* they have drawn, and *before* they discard.

In connection with adding cards to sets and sequences already face up on the table, there is a way of playing that is good fun to use. Suppose that you have a card that can be added to a set or sequence. And suppose, then, that you do not notice this fact, and discard the card, putting it on the face-up pile in the center of the table. Your opponent, if he spots what has happened, can call out "Rummy," pick up the card that you discarded, and add it to the set or sequence it belongs with. Then he can discard one of his own cards right away. He then goes on to play as though nothing had happened—drawing a card and discarding another card.

The game continues until one player gets rid of his last card. When he discards it, he shouts "Rummy," and the game is ended. After that the other player may not lay down or discard any more cards.

If no one has won before the center pile is used up, the pile is turned face down again, without being shuffled, and the game goes on until somebody wins.

Some players, who like to take risks, prefer to keep all their cards in their hands, without laying down any sets or sequences—hoping that they will be able to lay down their entire hand at one time and win the game all at once. When a player does this, it is called a "spread," and the score is higher for this.

Scoring. The winner of each game is credited with all the points left in the hand of his opponent, counting each face card (Kings, Queens and Jacks) as 10, each Ace as 1, and the other cards their regular value. Each deal may be treated as a separate game, or the first player to make 100 points may be called the winner of a game.

If a player lays down a "spread," he scores double the count of his opponent's cards. Don't try too hard to get "spreads." You get caught out with a handful of cards much more often than you succeed in laying down all your cards at once.

When more than two people play, the game is played in the same way, with these very slight changes: When three or four people play, each one is dealt 7 cards, when five or six people play, each is dealt 6 cards. The dealer deals clockwise, giving the first card to the person on his left, who also plays first, and is the next dealer. When there is a "spread," the winner earns double the count of the cards left in all the other players' hands.

TWO-TEN-JACK

This is a game a good deal like Rummy, in which you draw cards from a center pile, but it has a different method of scoring; which produces some surprising results. It is very popular in many parts of the country, and is played by both old and young. Two, three or four people can play.

The object of the game is to win certain cards that count *plus* or for you, in scoring, and to avoid taking cards that count *minus* or against you. These cards are as follows:

Two of Hearts, Ten of Hearts and Jack of Hearts—plus 10 points each.

Ace of Hearts, King of Hearts and Queen of Hearts—plus 5 points each.

Ace, King, Queen or Jack of Clubs and Diamonds—plus 1 point each.

Two of Spades, Ten of Spades and Jack of Spades—minus 10 points each.

Ace of Spades, King of Spades and Queen of Spades—minus 5 points each.

You can see at a glance that the Hearts are the good cards, and the Spades are the villains.

Hearts are *always* trumps in Two-Ten-Jack. In taking tricks, the cards rank from the Ace as the highest to the Two as the lowest. But for the purpose of taking a trick, the Ace of Spades is always the highest card of all. It scores minus 5, but it can usually be played to win a plus card that will offset this. It ranks higher than even the Ace of Hearts, and it may be used at any time as a trump, just as though it were a Heart. The Ace of Spades is called "Speculation."

The players cut for the deal, and the one who cuts the highest card is the dealer. He deals the cards 1 at a time and in turn, giving his opponent the first card, until each player has 6 cards. The dealer then puts the rest of the pack face up in the center of the table, as a center pile or stock pile. Some players prefer to put the stock pile face down, and this is permitted.

The dealer's opponent leads the first card, and the dealer plays another card on it to make a trick, which consists of 2 cards. A player must follow suit if he can. If he cannot, he *must* play a trump card—a Heart or the Ace of Spades. If he cannot follow suit or play a trump, he may play any card.

The higher card of the suit led wins a trick, unless a trump is played. Then *it* wins the trick. If two trumps are played, the higher one wins.

When a trump—a Heart—is led, the person who has the Ace of Spades may play it and take the trick, or may play a Heart, just as he wishes. But when a Spade is led, the holder of the

Ace of Spades must play it if he has no other Spade. He cannot consider the Ace of Spades as a Heart under these conditions.

The winner of each trick leads a card for the next one. But before he leads, he takes the top card of the center pile, and the other player takes the card beneath it.

The game goes on until the center pile has been used up and the cards remaining in the players' hands have been played out.

Then each player looks through his cards and picks out the ones that score plus and the ones that score minus. Each adds up his plus cards first and writes down their total. Then he adds up the minus cards and gets their total. The difference between the totals is his score. If a player totals more plus than minus points, he has a plus score. But if he has more minus points than plus ones, he has a minus score. Whatever it is, he writes it down as his score for the deal.

The winner of the game is the one who first scores 25 plus points.

If three people want to play Two-Ten-Jack, remove the Three of Clubs from the pack. Each player is dealt 6 cards, and the person on the dealer's left plays first. The winner of a trick takes the top card of the center pile, the player at his left the card beneath it, and the third player takes the next card.

When four people play, the entire pack is used and each player is dealt 6 cards. The game is then played just the same as for three players.

FIFTEEN

Fifteen is a game of chance for two people, in which each player draws cards from the pack and tries to get a total count of 15, without going over that total. You can learn it by playing one game with a friend, and you can then enjoy playing it for years.

The cards have a count as follows: Any Ace counts 1; any King, Queen or Jack counts 10; and the other cards have their regular values, a Two counting as 2, a Three as 3, and so on.

Before starting to play, each player puts an equal number of counters (buttons, beans, toothpicks, or other small objects) on the table. The number may be 2 or 3 or more; it doesn't matter. But each player must put out the same number.

The dealer shuffles the cards, then deals 1 card face down to his opponent, and 1 card face down to himself, and puts the rest of the pack face down on the table.

The dealer's opponent looks at his card. If he has a card that counts as 10, he may decide to "stand" and not draw another card. Or, whether he has a 10 or a lower card, he may decide to draw one or more other cards. He draws them 1 at a time, taking them from the top of the face-down pack. If he goes over 15, he stops drawing, but he does not tell the dealer.

The dealer then either "stands" or draws 1 or more cards. When he finishes drawing, both players show their hands, and the one whose cards total nearest 15, without going over it, wins the other player's counters.

If there is a tie or if both players go over 15, the counters are left on the table for the next deal. Each player, however, adds an equal number of new counters before the cards are dealt again. The players take turns dealing the cards for the tricks.

After each trick, the dealer takes the cards played and puts them to one side. He then continues the deal from the unused part of the pack. When the pack has been gone through, the dealer picks up all the cards and shuffles them before starting a new deal. The game continues as long as the players wish to keep on with it. At the end, the final winner is the one who has the most counters.

TWO-HANDED HEARTS

Hearts is so popular and so well-known that you may some-times want to play it when there are only two people to make up a game. This is easy to do, and is just as much fun as play-ing with the usual number of four. The object of the game is to avoid winning any Hearts, if you can. The rules are the same as those given for Hearts on page 83.

Either player deals first, and deals 13 cards each, one at a time and in turn, first 1 to his opponent, then 1 to himself, and so on. The rest of the pack is placed face down on the table, where both players can reach it.

The dealer's opponent leads, playing any card he wishes, by putting it face up on the table. The dealer must then fol-low suit if he can. If he cannot, he may play any card he chooses and usually will want to get rid of a Heart. The per-son who plays the highest card of the suit led wins the trick. He picks it up and puts it to one side.

The winner of each trick leads for the next one. But before doing so, he draws the top card from the face-down pile and adds it to his hand. The other player then takes the card now on top of the face-down pile, and the winner then leads for the next trick.

The game goes on until all the cards in the face-down pile have been drawn. The remaining 13 cards in each hand are then played, and the winner is the player who has the fewest Hearts in the tricks he has taken.

WAR

This is a wonderful game for beginners, because it is so easy to play. But make no mistake; it is just as exciting as many other harder and more complicated games.

War is usually played by two people, but three, four or more can play it. I will describe the two-handed game first, and then tell how to play when there are more players.

Either player may deal. He gives the cards out face down, one at a time, first one to his opponent, then one to himself, and so on. Each player then puts his cards face down in a pile in front of him, without looking at them.

The object of the game is to win the other player's cards by turning up cards of higher rank or value. The player who captures all the cards is the winner.

The Ace is the highest card, followed by the King, Queen, and the other cards down to the Two, which is the lowest card.

The game is started by each player's picking up the top card of his pile and putting it face up on the table. The turned-up cards are put right in front of each player's pile.

Whoever plays the higher card—even if it is a different suit—takes both cards and puts them, face down, at the bottom of his pile.

Each player turns up another card, and the higher card wins. This is kept up, turn after turn.

The excitement starts when both players play cards of the same value, such as 2 Aces or 2 Fives. Then a War starts at once. The 2 like cards are left on the table. Each player plays another card, *face down*, partly covering the first one, and a third card, *face up*, partly covering the second one (Fig. 16). The higher of the last 2 cards takes all 6 cards, and the winner puts them face down at the bottom of his pile.

If the last two face-up cards of the 6 are also of the same value, there is a Continued War. Each player must play another *face-down* card and another *face-up* card (Fig. 16) and the winner takes all 10 cards.

The game continues until one of the players has captured all the cards and is the winner.

When three people play, remove a Two from the pack and deal each player 17 cards. Then you have War whenever any two players turn up cards of the same value, and the winner takes the cards of both the other players.

WAR

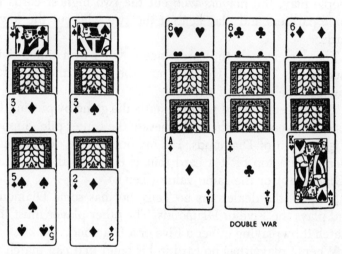

CONTINUED WAR

DOUBLE WAR

Fig. 16

If all three players turn up cards of the same value, you have a Double War. Each player plays 2 cards face down, and then 1 card face up, as shown in Fig. 16.

When four people play, you use the whole pack and each player gets 13 cards. There is Double War if all players turn up cards of the same value.

If more than four people play, take enough cards from the pack to give each player the same number of cards.

CRAZY EIGHTS

Two people usually play Crazy Eights, but it is also often played by four people who play in partnerships, two against two. A larger number may play, but if they do, each one plays for himself, and tries to get rid of his cards as fast as he can, for that is the object of the game.

The cards are cut to see who will be the dealer, and the person who cuts the lowest card deals. In Crazy Eights, the Ace is the lowest card, ranking below a Two. When four people play, the players who cut the two highest cards become partners and play against the two who cut the lowest cards.

The dealer deals the cards face down 1 at a time, giving each player 7 cards. He then puts the rest of the pack face down in the center of the table.

The player who did not deal starts the game by putting 1 of his cards face up on the table, beside the center pile. Suppose it is the Ten of Diamonds. His opponent (the dealer) must then put on top of it a card that is either of the same suit (Diamonds) or the same value (Ten).

Suppose the dealer has no Tens, but has some Diamonds, and plays the Five of Diamonds. The other player must then match it by playing either a Five or a Diamond.

When a player has no card in his hand that can match the card just played, he draws cards one at a time from the center pile until he gets one he can play, or even longer, if he likes.

The 4 Eights are "crazy" or "wild", and can be played at any time. When an Eight is played, it can be called any suit. For example, a Two of Clubs has just been played. The other player then plays an Eight of Hearts, but as he puts it down, he says "Clubs" to show that he is using it to match the Two of Clubs.

When all the cards in the center pile have been used up, the players must do the best they can with the cards in their hands. If one of them cannot play, he says "Pass" and the other player puts down another card. This may be any card that he has in his hand.

The game keeps on until one player has gotten rid of all of his cards by playing them, or until a player puts down a card that neither his opponent nor himself can match and play on.

When four people are playing, in partnerships, the player at the dealer's left plays the first card. The game then goes on even after one player has played all his cards. It continues as long as players on opposite sides remain in the game.

The winner scores for the cards that remain in his opponent's hand. An Eight counts 50 points; a King, Queen, Jack or Ten counts 10 points; an Ace counts 1 point; and all the other cards count their regular values.

The first player to make 500 points is the final winner of a game. Some players, however, like to make game 100 points. Either way is all right.

If, as sometimes happens, a game ends with both players still holding some cards in their hands, the player whose cards add up to the lowest total of points is the winner. He subtracts his points from those of his opponent, and the difference between the two counts as his score. When four people play, the points of the cards still held by each pair of partners are added up. The partners with the lowest number of points win. They subtract their points from those of the other two partners, and the difference between the two counts is their score.

There is one odd rule for Crazy Eights that you find in few other card games. This is that when a player draws cards from the center pile, he is allowed to keep on taking cards as long as he likes, even after he gets a card that he can play. Many beginners think this is a strange thing to do, since the object of the game is to get rid of your cards.

After you have played Crazy Eights a few times, however, you will see that it is sometimes an advantage to draw a number of cards. A player may draw cards, for example, in the hope of getting an Eight, which he can get rid of instantly at any time. Or he may draw cards to try to get most of the remaining cards of one suit such as, for example, Hearts. If he is successful, he can play his Hearts and his opponent may be unable to match them. The opponent may then have to draw a large number of cards before he gets one he can play.

POUNCE

Pounce is a double solitaire game, and is usually played by two people, although three, four or even more may play if the table is big enough to accommodate them all.

Each player has his own pack of cards and at the signal "Go!" each one starts to lay out his cards to begin a game of Klondike (see page 11). Each person plays as fast as he can, since the winner of the game is the one who first gets rid of all his cards, if possible; or otherwise the one who gets rid of the most cards.

All the Aces are put in the center to be the bottom cards of foundation piles where both players can reach them easily and build up other cards on them. Both players put cards on all the foundation piles—those of the opponent as well as their own, until no more plays are possible, or until one player has used up all his cards.

The cards held in their hands may be dealt on the table 1 at a time or 3 at a time. This must be decided before the game starts.

One of the best things about Pounce is that you are allowed to go through the cards in your hand as many times as you want to. You just keep on playing until you have managed to get rid of all the cards in your hand by playing them on the layout cards or the foundation piles, unless, in the meantime, your opponent has used up all his cards.

In addition to Klondike, you can play Pounce with Canfield (see page 8) or any other solitaire in which the four Aces are put out in the center to build on.

CASINO

Casino keeps going right on year after year as one of the most popular of all two-hand card games for both grownups and young people. It is easy to learn and play, and offers a great many opportunities for skillful play once you are familiar with it and have acquired a certain degree of expertness. That is one reason why Casino is a favorite with people of all ages.

In playing Casino, the Ace is valued as 1, the Two as 2, and so on up through the Ten. The Jack, Queen and King have no point value.

The dealer is chosen by cutting the cards, and the one who cuts the lowest card deals the first hand.

The dealer first gives his opponent 2 cards face down. He puts the next 2 cards side by side face up in the center of the table. Then he deals himself 2 cards face down. The same kind of deal is repeated. Each player then has 4 cards, and there are 4 cards face up in a row on the table.

The objects of the game are to take in as many cards as you can—over 27 if possible; to take in Spades; to take in Aces; the Two of Spades, which is called Little Casino; and the Ten of Diamonds, which is called Big Casino.

The player who did not deal starts the game by playing one card. He may do any one of four things—*take in, build, increase a build* or *trail.* Each of these must be carefully explained, so you will know just how the game works.

TAKING IN

1. If a player has a card in his hand of the same value as a card on the table, he may take in the card on the table. He puts both cards face down in front of him. Cards he takes in later are added to this pile.

Suppose you have a Seven in your hand and there is a Seven face up on the table. You put your Seven on the Seven on the table, and then pick up both cards and take them in.

2. If there are 2 cards of the same value on the table, a player may take them both with 1 card of the same value from his hand.

For example, if you have a Ten in your hand, and there are 2 Tens face up on the table, you show your Ten and take in both the other Tens, adding them to your pile.

3. A player may take in several cards whose values add up to the value of a card in his hand.

Suppose you have an Eight in your hand, and there are an Ace, a Three and a Four on the table. You can take in these 3 cards, whose values add up to 8, with your Eight.

It is usually a good idea to take in several cards at one time if you can, since one object of the game is to get 27 of the cards.

4. A player may take in, at one and the same time, a card of the same value as that of a card in his hand, and several other cards whose values add up to the value of the same card in his hand.

If you have an Eight, for example, you can take in an Ace, Three and Four, as above. If there is also an Eight on the table, you can take it in too.

5. A player often has a choice as to which card in his hand he can play. Suppose there are 2 Threes on the table and you have a Three and a Six in your hand. You may take both Threes with the Three in your hand, or you may take both Threes with the Six in your hand.

6. The face cards (King, Queen, Jack) are played a little differently. You may take only one face card from the table with a face card of the same value in your hand. Said another way, a face card may be used only to take in a like face card —and only 1 at a time.

If, for example, there are 2 Kings on the table and you have a King in your hand, you may take in only 1 of the Kings.

7. If, however, there are 3 face cards of the same value, such as 3 Kings, on the table, and you have the fourth King in your hand, you may take in the 3 other Kings all at one time.

BUILDING

There are two methods of building. These are called the "single build" and the "multiple build."

1. *Single Build.* To make a single build, you put a card from your hand on 1 or more cards on the table and say that you are building to a certain number. This number is always the value of a card that you hold in your hand.

For example, suppose there are a Two and a Three on the table, and you have in your hand an Ace and a Six. You put the Ace with the Two and the Three in a pile and say "I am building Six." This tells your opponent that you have a Six in your hand.

Your object in making a single build is to take in the cards the next time you play, and the rules say that you must do this. But if your opponent, in the example given above, also has a Six, he may take in your build and get it away from you. Your opponent is not permitted to take in separately any of the cards that have been designated as a build. He must take in the complete build or leave the cards alone. The face cards cannot be used in building.

2. *Multiple Build.* The best way to illustrate a multiple build is by an example. Suppose there is a Five on the table and you have 2 Fives in your hand. You put 1 of your Fives on the Five on the table and say, "Building Fives." On your next turn, you take in the multiple build (the 2 Fives) with your remaining Five.

If there are other cards on the table that add up to 5, you may take them in at the same time.

You are not allowed to use the face cards in multiple building. If there is a Jack on the table and you have 2 Jacks in your hand, you may not "build Jacks."

INCREASING A BUILD

Increasing your builds is quite a tricky and fascinating business. If you have your wits about you, you can use this method very successfully to build up your final score. There are two ways to increase a build, as follows:

1. You may increase a single build you have started, when your next turn comes, by making another single build and adding it to the first one. Suppose, for example, that you have built Six, as in the example given above under *Single Build*. You notice a Four on the table and you have a Two in your hand. You may then put your Two on the Four to make another Six, and add these cards to your first Six build. This makes a multiple build of Sixes, which you will take in the next time you play.

2. You may increase a single build by adding a card to it from your hand to give it a higher value. Say that you have built Six. You see in your hand a Two and an Eight. You may then add the Two to your Six build and say, "Building Eight," planning to take in the build on your next turn. This is a method by which you can often take in more cards.

Your opponent may also increase one of your own single builds in this way. If he sees your Six build and has, for example, a Three and a Nine in his hand, he may add the Three and say, "Building Nine." He will then get the build away from you at his next turn unless you too happen to have a Nine and can take it in yourself.

3. Multiple builds stay as they are. You are not allowed to increase their value to the combined value of the cards they contain. For example, if a player is "Building Twos" and has added a Two from his hand to a Two on the table, his opponent may not take in the build with a Four.

4. To increase a build, you must add a card from your hand. You are not allowed to use cards from the table.

A player must take in his own build on his next turn, unless he chooses to (1) make another build, (2) take in a card or a combination of cards as described under *Taking In,* or (3) take his opponent's build. This gives you wide freedom of play.

The only thing you are not allowed to do when you have a build on the table is to trail, which is described as follows.

TRAILING

A player trails when he does not take in cards or make a build, and he does so by putting a card face up on the table beside the other cards. This generally means that he is unable to play, but not always. If a player has 2 scoring cards such as 2 Aces or 2 Twos including Little Casino (the Two of Spades), he will often trail one card and take it in with the other on his next turn. It is wisest to play a small card when you trail. Never play an Ace or Little Casino if you can avoid it.

You are allowed to trail whenever you wish to, except when you have a build on the table. Then you must take in the build on your next turn.

PLAYING THE GAME

After the cards are first dealt, the player who is not the dealer starts the game by taking in 1 or more cards, making a build or trailing. When he has done all he can, the dealer has his turn, and the turns then alternate until each player has played out his first 4 cards.

The dealer then deals 4 more cards to his opponent and himself, using the same method as in the first deal. He does not now or at any later deal, however, put any more cards face up on the table.

The game continues until all the cards in the pack have been dealt out.

After both players have played out their hands in the last deal, any cards that remain on the table belong to the player who was the last to take in any cards. He puts them on his pile so he can add them to his score.

SCORING

Each player looks through the cards he has taken in. Both count the number of cards, the number of Spades, and the number of Aces they have. Then the points that each player has won are added up. The points that count are as follows:

	Points
Cards, for taking 27 or more cards	3
Spades, for taking 7 or more spades	1
Big Casino (Ten of Diamonds)	2
Little Casino (Two of Spades)	1
Aces, for each Ace taken in	1
Sweeps, for each	1

A sweep is scored whenever a player takes all the cards on the table with one card from his hand. In case of a tie, the side winning "cards" (27 or more) is considered the winner.

The winner is the player who first makes a score of 21 points. If both players reach 21 or more points in the same deal, the one who has the higher score is the winner.

POINTS ON PLAYING CASINO

It is best to take in low cards from the table, if you can, for this leaves your opponent fewer low cards on which to make builds.

Try to keep track of how you are doing while taking in cards and Spades. Take in Spades whenever you can, to better your chances of getting 7 of them.

In the early part of the game, it is usually fairly safe to build with Aces, as there is not much chance that your opponent will get them away from you. It is considered that you have a better chance to keep your Aces by building with them than by holding them back and trailing with some other card.

If you get Big Casino, the Ten of Diamonds, in your hand, do everything possible to keep it in your possession. Hold on until you can take in a Ten with it or build Ten.

Try to take in as many cards as you can, by combining cards on the table to match the value of a card in your hand. This adds to your card score, which you want to push up to 27 if you can.

STEALING THE OLD MAN'S BUNDLE

Many people who like to play Casino have never tried this similar and very interesting game. It is easier to play than Casino, and contains an added element of surprise, for your carefully collected "bundle," which may contain Big Casino or other scoring cards, may be stolen from you at any time. One of the best things about the game, however, is that you are often able to steal your "bundle" back again, together with some more scoring cards taken in by your opponent.

The cards are dealt and the game is played just like Casino, except that there is no building. The players take in and trail, but do not build. There is also one other difference, which is that when a player takes in some cards, he puts them in front of him, *face up*, instead of face down. These cards are his "bundle."

Now, whenever a player has a card of the same value as the top card of his opponent's bundle, he captures the whole bundle and puts it face up on his own bundle.

PERSIAN PASHA

Persian Pasha is an old, old game invented many hundreds of years ago in the Orient. It is one of the really good games for two players.

You do not have to cut for deal. Either player can take the pack, shuffle the cards, and start dealing them out alternately, one at a time—1 to his opponent, 1 to himself, 1 to his opponent, and so on until the entire pack has been dealt. Each person then puts his cards in front of him, face down in a pile.

Both players now play at the same time. Each picks up the top card of his pile and puts it face up on the table in front of the pile. This is continued until both players turn up a card of the same suit. The player who has the higher card then wins all of the cards in his opponent's face-up pile.

In Persian Pasha, the Aces are counted as the highest cards, over-ranking the Kings. This, of course, makes the Twos the lowest ranking cards.

The game keeps on until one player wins all of the other player's cards or until 2 cards of the same suit cannot be turned up at the same time, which sometimes happens. The winner then is the one who has captured the larger number of cards and, if he wishes to, he may call himself a Persian Pasha.

ROLLING STONE

I have always had a good time playing Rolling Stone. It moves along at a fast clip and keeps everybody busy until someone finally wins by getting rid of all of his cards. It is a good game for two people, is played often with four, and can be played with any number up to six or eight. The game is also called Enflay.

When there are two, three or four players, only 32 cards are used. These are the Sevens, Eights, Nines, Tens, Jacks, Queens, Kings and Aces. The Aces rank as the highest cards.

When there are five players, the Sixes and Fives are added; and when six people play, the Fours and Threes are added. This will give each player 8 cards.

It is customary to cut for the deal when playing Rolling Stone, the player who cuts the highest card becoming the dealer. He gives each player 8 cards, dealing them as follows —3 cards to each player on the first round of the table, 2 cards to each player on the second round, and 3 cards to each player on the third round.

The player on the dealer's left starts the game by putting a card face up in the center of the table. It makes no difference at all what this card is. You can pick the first one you see and play it, since no judgment is involved in your choice.

The next player to the left and the others that follow him all try to play a card of the same suit as the first one put on the table. If everybody can follow suit, the cards in the center of the table are picked up after all the players have added their cards, and are put to one side. Nobody scores anything.

The person who played the highest card in the first round then continues the game by putting one of his cards in the center of the table. Again, everybody tries to put on top of it a card of the same suit.

Before long some player will not be able to follow suit. When this happens he has to pick up all the cards in the center of the table at the time and add them to his hand. The players to his left, who ordinarily would have played their cards, do not put any cards out.

It is the player who had to pick up the cards who now starts a new round by putting a card in the center of the table. This card must always be of another suit than the cards he picked up. The game then keeps on in the same way until someone is able to get rid of all his cards. When this happens

the game comes to an end, even though some other player to the left of the winner would have been able to get rid of his last card if the round were finished.

The winner scores 1 point for each card that the other players hold in their hands at the end of the game. The scores should be written down with pencil and paper, as it is impossible to remember them when a number of games are played.

Why this game is called Rolling Stone has always puzzled me. The winner gets rid of his cards and so doesn't gather any moss that way; but just the same he collects a score, while the other players don't. Perhaps it is because the game rolls along at such a fast pace.

GIN RUMMY

Gin Rummy has become one of the most popular games in recent years, and if you don't already know how to play it, you can have a good time learning it now and playing it with a friend. It is most often played by two people, but can be played by three or four.

The cards are dealt out, 10 to each player, and the rest of the cards are put in the center of the table, exactly as in regular Rummy (See Fig. 15). Then you go ahead and play in the same way, the players alternately drawing a card from the center pile or the discard pile, playing, and then discarding a card.

Each player, just as in Rummy, tries to combine cards to make sets of 3 or 4 cards of the same number, such as 3 or 4 Fives or 3 or 4 Jacks.

Each player also tries to combine cards to make sequences of 3 or 4 cards of the same suit, such as the Two, Three and Four of Clubs, or the Three, Four, Five and Six of Hearts.

"KNOCKING"

But the players do not lay down their sets and sequences face up on the table, as they do in Rummy.

Instead, one player ends the play, after any deal, by "knocking."

A player can "knock" and end the play whenever he finds that the extra cards in his hand, outside of those combined in sets or sequences, and not counting the card he plans to discard, add up to 10 points or less.

This is a new principle to many card players, so I will try to make it absolutely clear by an example.

Fig. 17 shows a hand that permits the player to knock. It contains one set of 3 cards—3 Twos; and it contains a sequence of 3 cards—the Four, Five and Six of Diamonds. It also contains an extra card to discard. The remaining 4 cards add up to 10, so you can knock, and you are the winner for that particular deal.

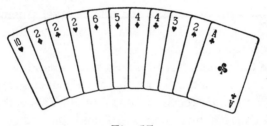

Fig. 17

I say "for that particular deal," because in Gin Rummy, you keep on playing until one player makes 100 points. The player who first makes 100 points wins the game.

Now, here are a few pointers—still about knocking—that should clear up everything that needs to be said on the subject:

1. A player may knock only after he has drawn a card and at the time he makes his *last* discard of a card for a hand.

2. The usual way of showing that you knock is to discard your last card face down—instead of face up as with all the other cards you put on the discard pile.

3. A player does not have to knock the first time his extra cards total 10 points or less. He may wait and try to get a lower total, if he wants to. Many players do this because the lower the total of these points, the higher is their score. You will see why this is so when you read about the scoring.

4. After a player knocks, he shows his sets and sequences, and announces the total of the points on his extra cards.

The other player then shows his sets and sequences and—remember this point—he sees if he can add any of his extra cards to the sets or sequences held by the winner. If he can get rid of one or more of his cards in this way, he does so.

All of this will be easy for you after you play a hand or two.

SCORING

1. To figure the score, the points of each player's extra cards are totaled. The score the winner receives is the difference between his points and the other player's points.

Each King, Queen, Jack or Ten is counted as 10, each Ace as 1, each other card its regular value.

Suppose the winner has 10 points, with a hand like the one shown in Fig. 17, and suppose the other player's extra cards total 20. The winner receives a score of 10. This is the difference between his own points—10—and the other player's points—20. You subtract the winner's points from the other player's points to get the winner's score.

2. It happens quite often in Gin Rummy that after the knocker puts his sets and sequences on the table, his opponent adds a number of his cards to them. By doing this, the opponent often reduces the total points of his extra cards so that they are equal to or less than those of the knocker.

If both player's points are equal, neither scores.

But if the opponent reduces his points so that they are equal to or less than those of the knocker, he becomes the winner and is the only one to score. He scores the difference in points between the two hands, *plus* a bonus of 10 points. This is called an "undercut" bonus, because it is earned by "cutting under" the knocker's points.

GIN

If a player can knock with a hand in which all 10 cards are combined into sets or sequences, he scores a "gin." For this he earns a 20-point bonus, plus the total points of the extra cards in the other player's hand.

The other player is allowed to add cards to the knocker's cards, and so reduce the point total of his hand. But even if he gets rid of all his extra cards in this way, he receives no score. The player who declared gin gets 20 points, and that is the scoring for that deal.

SCORING FOR AN ENTIRE GAME

At the end of each deal or hand, the winner writes down his score. The scores should be added together as the game goes along, so that each player can see how close he is getting to 100 points. The first player to get 100 points is the winner of the game. His score for the game is the difference between his points and his opponent's points.

When the game is finished, there are some extra scores to be figured.

Each player receives 20 points for every deal or hand he wins. This is called a box bonus.

The winner receives a game bonus of 100 points.

The winner receives a game bonus of 200 points, if his opponent scored not a single point during the game. This is called a shutout.

To make the scoring clear, here is a sample score for a game:

Sample Score

BOB	BILL
20	26
48	48
68	70
88	
108	

Bob won the first deal or hand by 20 points. Then he won the second deal by 28 points for a total score of 48 points.

Bill won the next two deals, capturing 26 points on the first, and 22 on the second for a total of 48.

Bob won the next two deals, getting 20 points on the first for a total of 68; and 20 points on the second for a total of 88. Then Bill won a deal and got 22 points, which brought his total score up to 70. But on the next deal Bob won 20 points, giving him a total of 108, and making him the winner.

Now, for the final game score:

Bob got 5 box bonuses, with 20 points each, or 100 points. Bill got 3 box bonuses, with 60 points. Bob receives credit for the difference between the two figures. This is 100 minus 60, or 40 points.

Bob scores the difference between the game points, 108 minus 70. This gives him 38 points.

Bob also gets a game bonus of 100 points. His total score for the game is written down as follows:

Bob's Score	Points
Difference in box bonuses	40
Difference in game points	38
Game bonus	100
Bob's total score for game	178

POINTS ON PLAYING GIN RUMMY

1. If you draw cards from the center pile until only 2 cards are left in it, you stop playing and call that deal or hand a draw. Neither player scores.

2. Your chief object in playing Gin Rummy is very different from your object in regular Rummy. Do not try mainly to make sets or sequences. Try always to reduce the count of your extra cards below 10. Be *sure* to remember this.

3. Don't keep trying to score a "gin." The chances of getting "gin" are small. It is almost always best to knock as soon as you can.

4. Always do all you can to collect low extra cards. Get rid of high extra cards quickly. Remember that the Ace is the lowest of all the cards. It counts only 1 in Gin Rummy, and is considered the most valuable card to have.

14 Games for Three or Four Players

Most of the games in this section are easy to play and can be learned in a few minutes. They include some of the very best of all the card games—old favorites that have whiled away the hours for millions of people, young and old.

You will probably know one or two of these games already. I hope you will try some of the ones you don't know the next time you and some of your friends want to have some fun with cards.

While most of the games in this section are usually played by four people, most of them can just as well be played by three. Some of them can be played by larger numbers than four, and a few can be played by two. Where this is the case, it is indicated in the description of the game.

TWENTY-NINE

Twenty-Nine can be played by any number of people from two to eight. It is one of the best of the easy-to-play card games, and you and your friends can learn it by playing a single hand or trick.

It is a good game for four people, playing as partners, two against two. But it is also good fun with three, four, five or even more players, each one playing for himself.

The dealer is the person who cuts the highest card. All the cards in the pack are dealt to the players, face down and one at a time, the first card going to the player on the dealer's left. After the first hand has been played, the person on the dealer's left becomes the dealer. The person on his left follows him as dealer, and so on around the table.

In Twenty-Nine, all the face cards (Kings, Queens and Jacks) count only as 1. The other cards have their regular value, the Aces counting as 1, the Twos as 2, the Threes as 3, and so on.

The object of the game is to win as many cards as possible, by reaching the exact total of 29, as described below.

The player at the dealer's left starts the game by putting a card face up in the center of the table and calling out its value. Each player then adds a card, in turn, and as he does so, he calls out the total value of all the cards played up to that time. You do not have to follow suit, but may play any card at all.

For example, the first player puts down a Six, and calls out "Six." The second player puts down a Two, and calls out "Eight"—the total value of the Six and the Two. The third player puts down a Seven and calls out "Fifteen"—the total of 8 and 7.

The winner of a hand is the person who plays a card that brings the total exactly to 29. He picks up the cards on the table and puts them face down in front of him, keeping them until all of the cards have been played and it is time to count up the score.

The game is continued by the player at the left of the winner, who starts a new round by putting a card face up in the middle of the table.

No one is ever allowed to play a card that will make the total more than 29. Otherwise he must play each time it is his turn. If someone is unable to play without making the total more than 29, he says "Pass" and the person at his left plays a card. If a player runs out of cards, he is out of the game until there is another deal.

When all the cards have been played, everybody adds up

the points of the cards he has won, and the person or partnership with the highest total is the winner.

If some of the cards are left on the table because it was not possible to complete the last round by making a total of 29, those cards are left out of the scoring.

So that each person will receive the same number of cards, it is customary in playing Twenty-Nine to remove some cards from the pack, according to the number of players, and this rule is usually followed: If two or four people play, use the whole pack. If three people play, remove 1 of the Tens. If five people play, remove 2 of the Tens. If six or eight people play, remove all 4 Tens. If seven people play, remove 3 of the Tens.

STAY AWAY

The thing about Stay Away that makes it different from many other card games is that, instead of taking tricks, you do everything you can not to take them. The Jacks are the villains of the game. They are the cards you absolutely, positively don't want.

Four is the best number of players, and each one plays for himself. The game can be played, however, by any number from three to six.

The idea of the game is to avoid taking any trick containing a Jack, and to have the lowest score when some player ends the game by scoring 10 against himself. The only cards counted in the scoring are the Jacks, and they count against you. The Jack of Spades counts 3 points, and each of the other Jacks 1 point.

When four people play, use only the 32 highest cards—the Aces, Kings, Queens, Jacks, Tens, Nines, Eights and Sevens. Anybody can be the first dealer. The dealer gives each player 8 cards, dealing 3 to each player, then 2, and then 3.

The player on the dealer's left starts the game by leading any card. The other players must then follow suit if they can.

If a player fails to follow suit when he can, he has 1 point marked against him.

The highest card of the suit led wins the trick, and the winner of each trick leads for the next one. The Ace counts as the highest card in taking tricks.

In the early part of the game, the best thing to do is to lead cards that are lower than the Jack. If you lead a higher card such as a Queen, a King, or an Ace, someone may play a Jack, and you will be forced to take it in.

When all the cards have been played, everyone looks through his cards and writes down his score against himself. This is reckoned by the Jacks he has had to take.

The cards are then shuffled and the player to the left of the original dealer deals them for the next round, and the deal passes in turn to the left.

The score is not added up until the end of each round, each time the cards are all played. The game ends when some player at the end of a round—but not before—has 10 points against him as a total of the rounds played. The player with the lowest score is then the winner. If two players tie, each having the same low score, another round is played so that one of them may be the clear-cut winner.

When five people play, add the Fives and Sixes to the 32 high cards to make a total of 40 cards. When six play, use the whole pack except for the 4 Twos. This makes a pack of 48 cards, and each player is dealt 8 cards.

FROGS IN THE POND

This is easy and interesting to play, but you have to keep your mind on the game pretty well to win, because you have to keep track of the high cards and remember which ones have been played.

Four people playing as partners, two against two, are the best number for Frogs, but it can be played by any number from two to six.

When there are four players, remove 2 of the Twos from the pack. The dealer deals the cards 2 at a time until each player has 10 cards. He then deals the next 10 cards face down to make a pile, and puts the pile in the center of the table. These are the Frogs in the Pond.

The object of the game is to be the first to score 100 points by winning cards that count in the scoring.

Each Ten	10 points
Each Five	5 points
Each Ace	4 points
Each King	3 points
Each Queen	2 points
Each Jack	1 point

Each trick is won by the highest card of the suit led, and the Ace ranks as the highest card in winning tricks. Then the King, Queen, Jack and so on, down to the Two.

The players must follow suit if they can. If a player "revokes," or fails to follow suit when he can, he loses 10 points from his score. When a player cannot follow suit, he may play any card.

The player to the left of the dealer starts the game by leading a card, placing it face up in the center of the table. The best strategy, when you are playing partners, is to lead an Ace. Then, if your partner has a Ten or a Five or some other scoring card, he can put it on your Ace and your side will win both cards.

The winner of each trick picks up the cards won and, at the same time, takes the top card of the Frogs pile. He looks at this card, but he must take care that no one else, not even his partner, sees it. He does not add it to his hand, but puts it face down with the cards he has just won. If it is a scoring card, it will count for him. He then leads for the next trick.

Each winner of a trick always does the same thing—takes a Frog to add to the cards won.

When all the cards have been played, each side adds up its

score and writes it down. The cards are then shuffled and dealt again, the new dealer being the player to the left of the previous dealer.

The first side to score 100 points wins the game. If four people are playing independently, each for himself, the first player to score 100 points is the winner.

When three people want to play Frogs in the Pond, use the whole pack and deal 13 cards to each player and 13 cards to the Frogs pile. When five people play, remove the 4 Twos, and deal 8 cards to each player and 8 cards to the Frogs pile. Each player must always have the same number of cards as the Frogs in the Pond.

AUTHORS

The game of Authors gets its name from the fact that the aim of the players is to collect "books" of cards. A "book" consists of a set of 4 cards of the same value, such as 4 Aces, 4 Fives or 4 Kings. It can be played by any number of people from three to six.

The cards are dealt out, face downward, one to each player in turn until the entire pack is dealt. If the cards do not come out evenly so that everyone has the same number, it doesn't matter.

The object of each player now is, as stated above, to collect "books" of 4 cards of the same value, such as 4 Aces, 4 Fives or 4 Kings.

The person sitting at the dealer's left begins the game. He turns to one of the other players and asks for a card of a certain value. For example, he says, "Please give me a Five." Of course, he asks for a card that will help to make a "book."

The player who is asked for the card must give the asker all the cards he has of the required value. If he has 2 Fives, for example, he hands them over. If he has 3 Fives, he has to hand them all over.

The first player is allowed to keep on asking different

people for cards just as long as he is successful in getting the cards he asks for. When he asks someone for a card, and the other player does not have any cards of that value, the turn of the first player comes to an end.

The person sitting at the left of the first player then starts to ask for cards, and keeps on until he is met with a refusal. The turn then goes to the player at his left, and so on around the table.

As soon as a player succeeds in getting a "book" of 4 cards of the same value, he has to show them to the other players and put them face down in front of him on the table.

Little by little, the cards will match up and before long all the cards will be arranged together in "books," and all will be lying face down on the table. The game ends at that point, and the player who has the largest number of "books" is the winner.

There are two or three simple rules that must be observed, since they will clear up points that may come up while you are playing:

1. You are not allowed to ask for a card unless you already have at least one card of the same value in your hand.

2. You must show a "book" as soon as it is completed. If you don't you are not allowed to count it in your score.

3. If you have a card in your hand, and another player asks you for it, you have to hand it over. No fair holding back.

The game may also be played by having each player ask for a special card, naming both its value and its suit. He must say, for example, "Please give me the Two of Hearts," or "Please give me the Seven of Clubs." He can continue asking as long as he is successful in getting cards. This method, of course, makes playing a little more difficult.

GO FISH!

Go Fish is played a good deal like Authors, but some people think it is more fun because it has a little more variety of action, and you get the chance every so often to tell some other player to "Go Fish!"

Any number from three to six or eight may play.

The cards are dealt out one at a time, but each player is given 5 cards only. The rest of the pack is put in the center of the table, face down, and becomes a center pile.

The player at the dealer's left starts the game by asking any other player for a card of a certain value, such as a Six or a Ten, which will help him to make a "book" of 4 cards of the same value. The asking player must always hold in his own hand at least one card of the value he asks for.

If the player who is asked for the card has it, he hands it over. The first player may then ask anyone at the table for another card, and another, as long as he is successful in getting cards. But if the player who is asked for a card doesn't have it, he tells the other player to "Go Fish!"

The asking player then picks up the top card of the center pile. If this card completes a "book," he puts the "book" face down on the table and goes on asking for cards. If, however, the card he draws does not complete a "book," he adds the card to those in his hand, his turn comes to an end, and the person on his left starts to ask for cards.

The game is sometimes played with the rule that if the asking player draws from the top of the center pile the card he last asked for, he may go on asking for cards. If he does not get such a card, his turn comes to an end.

LAST IN

This is one of the games in which the players draw cards from a center pile and play them to the center of the table. Its most novel feature is that the players are forced to drop out one by one as they run out of cards, and the winner is the one who holds out the longest and is the "last in."

Four players is the best number for Last In, but it can be played by from three to six people.

The players cut for the deal and the person who cuts the highest card is the dealer. He deals the cards one at a time, starting with the player on his left. If four people are playing, he gives each one 6 cards. When three people play, each one gets 7 cards; when five play, each one gets 5 cards; and when six play, each one gets 4 cards.

When the dealer deals himself his last card, he turns it face up. Its suit is the trump for the hand just dealt.

The dealer then puts the rest of the pack face down in the center of the table, where it becomes a center pile from which the players can draw.

The object of the game is to take as many tricks as possible in order to remain in the game until the end, for each time a player takes a trick he may add a card to his hand.

The player at the dealer's left starts by playing one of his cards—it does not matter which one. The other players, as their turns come, must play a card of the same suit if they can. If a player cannot follow suit, he may play a trump card, but he does not have to. It depends upon his judgment and the course of the game. He may play any other card in his hand if he cannot follow suit and does not want to play a trump.

The person who plays the highest card of the suit of the first card wins the trick, unless a trump is played. An Ace, in Last In, is the highest card, outranking a King, but a trump card always wins. If more than one trump is played the highest trump takes the trick.

The person who wins a trick continues the game by leading or putting a card in the center of the table. Before he does this, however, he takes the top card of the center pile and adds it to his hand, without letting anyone else see it. The other players do not draw cards. This is because the aim of each player is to collect cards from the center pile, which will enable him to stay in the game longer; and to collect these cards he has to win tricks. Every time he loses, he comes closer to the point at which he will run out of cards and will have to drop out of the game.

As the game continues, the players will begin to drop out as they come to the end of their cards. The winner is the one who still has one or more cards left after everybody else has run out of cards.

DONKEY

Donkey is a fast and uproarious game. There is really no other card game quite like it. It can be played by any number of people from three up, but usually is the most fun when there are four to six players.

Before you start to play, remove from the pack 4 cards of the same value for each player in the game. Most often, the 4 Aces, 4 Kings, 4 Queens, 4 Jacks or 4 Tens are removed, in that order. If there are more than five players, you can remove, in addition, the 4 Nines, the 4 Eights, and as many other sets of 4 like cards as you need.

To make this absolutely clear, I will say it in another way. Suppose that three people are playing. You would then remove from the pack the 4 Aces, the 4 Kings, and the 4 Queens. This would make a complete set of 4 like cards for each of the three players. If four people are playing, you would remove the 4 Aces, 4 Kings, 4 Queens and 4 Jacks.

The cards that are removed are put together and well shuffled. The rest of the cards are put to one side, for they are not used in the game.

Now, still before starting to play, you put some counters in the middle of the table. These may be buttons, checkers, matches, toothpicks, pebbles, beans or any other handy objects. The number of counters is one less than the number of players. If there are four players, for example, 3 counters are put on the table.

The object of the game is to avoid being the Donkey, and to do this you have to grab one of the counters when the proper time comes.

Any player starts to deal, and the deal passes each time to the person on the left.

The dealer deals the cards one at a time to each player around the table, until everybody has a hand of 4 cards.

The game then gets under way, and each player tries to be the first to get 4 cards all of the same value.

The dealer starts the game by saying "Go!" Everyone then starts to pass cards, one at a time, to the person on his left.

If you have 2 cards of the same value, such as 2 Jacks, you try to get a third, and then the fourth Jack as fast as you can. Everybody passes cards continuously and as fast as possible.

As soon as a player gets 4 cards of the same value, he cries "Donkey!" and grabs for a counter. Then every other player grabs for a counter too.

One player is bound to miss out, as there are not enough counters to go around, and he is immediately called the "Donkey."

Donkey is a fast-moving game, and you usually play a number of games, one right after the other. When you do this, the first player who becomes a donkey 10 times is called the

"Prize Donkey" and has to show the others how well he can "Hee-haw."

Another way of playing is to give a letter of the word "Donkey," to each player who loses a game. Bill loses a game and gets a "d"; then Jane loses a game and also gets a "d". The next time either Bill or Jane loses a game he gets the letter "o", and so on. The first player to get the full word "Donkey" is the loser, and has to "Hee-haw" as long as the others want him to.

SLAPJACK

If you have never played Slapjack, now is the time to begin. There is quite a bit of noise and excitement to it, and it is good fun. Three or more people usually play, and each one is out for himself. Two people can play if they want to.

The dealer deals out all the cards in the pack one at a time and face down, starting with the player at his left. It does not matter if players don't all have the same number of cards. No one is allowed to look at any of his cards. Each player puts his cards face down, in a pile in front of him.

The idea of the game is to see who can win the most cards by putting his hand on a Jack when it is played onto a pile in the center of the table. The game usually keeps on until someone has captured all the cards.

The first player is the person on the dealer's left. He turns up the top card of his pile, with its face away from him so that he cannot see it, and puts it face up in the center of the table. The player at his left then does the same, and so on around the table. Everyone plays quickly, bang, bang, bang, one right after the other.

Whenever a Jack is put on the center pile, everybody tries to slap it by putting his hand on it. Players must play and slap with the same hand. No fair using both hands. The first person to get his hand on the Jack wins the Jack and all the cards that are beneath it. If two players each think they are the first to slap a Jack all the players must argue it out between them and agree somehow on which player got there first. The hand at the bottom, right next to the Jack, is the winner.

When a player wins a group of cards by slapping a Jack, he shuffles them into the pile of cards in front of him. The person at his left then continues the game by putting the top card of his pile on the center pile.

Sometimes a player uses up all the cards in his pile. If that happens, he watches the others and tries to be the first to slap the next Jack. If he succeeds, he goes on playing with the cards he captures. But if he does not succeed, he must drop out of the game until the next deal.

It sometimes happens that a player will get excited and slap the center pile when there is no Jack on top of it. Whoever does this must pick up the top card of his pile and give it to the person who last put a card on the center pile.

The game keeps on, as I said at the beginning, until one player succeeds in capturing all the cards.

SNAP

Snap is played a good deal like Slapjack, but is not so well known. It is just as much fun and requires the players to be, if possible, even more alert than when playing Slapjack.

In Snap, all the cards are dealt out exactly as in Slapjack, and each player puts his cards in front of him, face down in a pile.

The player to the left of the dealer starts the game by turning the top card of his pile face up and putting it on the table in front of his pile. He should turn the card away from him so that he does not see it before the other players do. The next player to the left then does the same thing, and so on around the table.

Each player watches the other players' face-up piles, and whenever someone turns up a card that is of the same value as a card on a face-up pile, each tries to be the first to call out "Snap." The player who first says "Snap" wins the face-up pile of the player on whose pile the first of the two similar cards was resting. He adds these to his own face-up pile and puts both piles face down on the bottom of his face-down cards.

The game keeps on until one player wins all the cards.

YUKON

In the days of the great Alaskan gold rush, Yukon was one of the most popular games played by the gold miners. A great many people still like its distinctive method of ranking the cards, in which the 4 Jacks are called Yukons, and the many surprises that come about as a result of these cards turning up during a game. The Yukons, 4 Jacks, count as the highest cards in the pack. The Jack of Spades is the Grand Yukon, and counts higher than the other 3 Jacks, all of which count the same.

Yukon is usually played by four people, who play in partnerships, two against two. It can also be played, however, by either two or three people, so don't hesitate to try it out with this smaller number, if you want to. Just remember that when three people play, you have to remove one of the Twos from the pack. When two or four people play, you use the whole pack.

The players cut for the deal, and the person cutting the highest card deals. He gives each player a hand of 5 cards, which are dealt around the table one at a time to each player. The first card goes to the player on the dealer's left, and the deal continues around the table to the left.

The dealer then puts the rest of the cards face down in the center of the table, where they become the center pile.

The object of the game is to win tricks containing certain counting cards and to be the first to win 250 points.

The cards that count in the scoring are:

Grand Yukon . . .	15 points
Each Yukon . . .	10 points
Each Ten	10 points
Each Ace	5 points
Each King	3 points
Each Queen . . .	2 points

The player at the dealer's left starts the game by putting a card face up in the center of the table. The other players in turn must then play cards of the same suit, if they are able to. If a player can't follow suit, he *must* play a Yukon if there is one in his hand. Otherwise, he plays any card. A Yukon is played *only* when its holder cannot follow suit, or when it is led.

Each hand or trick is won by the person who played the highest card of the suit established by the first card—except when someone plays a Yukon. In that case, the person who played the Yukon wins the hand. If more than one Yukon is played, the first one is the winner, unless the Jack of Spades, the Grand Yukon, is played. The Grand Yukon always wins, whether it is put down first or last. After the Jacks, the Aces are the next highest cards in winning tricks in the established suit. They are followed by the Kings, Queens, Jacks, and so on down to the Twos. The player that wins a hand picks up the cards and puts them in front of him face down so that he will be able to reckon up his score at the end of the game.

A player will sometimes lead a Yukon, hoping to win a hand. When this is done, the other players must match the suit of the Yukon if they can. But if a player has no cards of that suit, he *must* play a Yukon if he has one.

The player who wins a hand is the one who starts the next hand or leads for the next trick, by putting a card face up in the center of the table. Before he does this, however, he takes the top card of the center pile and adds it to his hand, taking care that none of the other players see it. Each of the other players, in his regular order from left to right around the table, then takes a card from the top of the center pile. This keeps five cards always in each player's hand.

The game keeps on until no more cards are left in the center pile. The players then use up the cards in their hands and the game comes to an end.

Each player or each pair of partners adds up his score and writes it down, using the values of the counting cards as given on page 81.

The cards are then dealt for the next round by the player to the left of the original dealer.

The first player or pair of partners to score 250 points is the winner. If two players or both partnerships have a score of 250 or more, the higher score wins. If the scores are exactly equal, as sometimes happens, the player or partnership that has the Ace of Spades at the end is the winner. The Ace of Spades is called the Yukon Digger, and sometimes comes in handy, as you can see.

The rule that makes Yukon such an exciting game is the one that says "Follow suit or play a Yukon." You must follow suit.

You are not allowed, for example, to play even the Grand Yukon as long as you can follow suit. And, if you *cannot* follow suit, you *must* play a Yukon if you have one.

Try out Yukon and think of the bearded miners of the old gold-rush days. You will have a mighty good time.

HEARTS

The popularity of Hearts seems to go right on year after year. It is played by families and at parties by both old and young, and it always keeps the players amused and interested. It is usually played by four people, but any number from two to six can play. The two-handed game is described in the section on "Card Games for Two Players."

In playing Hearts, if three people play, remove 1 black Two from the pack. If five play, remove 2 black Twos; and if six play, remove all 4 Twos.

The big idea in playing Hearts is to take just as *few* Hearts as possible. It is mostly a matter of luck, depending upon the cards you are dealt and the cards that are played by the others. But you have to watch the cards closely right along so as not to miss any opportunity to unload some of the Hearts in your hand.

The Ace is the highest card in Hearts, ranking above the King. This makes the Two the lowest card. When you cut to see who will be dealer, the player who cuts the lowest card deals the first hand. The turn to deal then goes around the table to the left.

The dealer gives each player one card at a time, starting with the person on his left. He deals out the entire pack, so that each player has 13 cards, if four persons are playing.

The game then starts by the person on the dealer's left playing a card. This may be any card at all in his hand. The next player to the left then plays a card and he and the two other players must follow suit if they can. If the first card played was a Diamond, for example, the other players must play Diamonds if they can.

If a player cannot follow suit, he may play a card of any other suit. That is how the players usually get rid of their Hearts. Out they go, at every chance that comes along to discard them.

When all four players have played a card, the cards on the table make up a trick. They are picked up by the person who played the highest card of the suit led by the first player. He puts them face down on the table in front of him.

The person who wins a trick is always the one who plays the next card or leads for the next trick, as card players say. He puts a card face up in the center of the table and the game goes on as before, each player following suit or playing a Heart or some other card, according to the cards he holds. The game goes on until everybody has played out all his cards.

At the end of a game, each player looks through the cards he has won as tricks to see how many Hearts he has. The scores are written down on a piece of paper, and each Heart counts 1 point.

People usually play until someone runs up a score of either 50 or 100. Then everybody's score is totaled, and the player with the lowest score is the final winner.

OLD MAID

Old Maid can be played by any number of people from three up. Most of the time four people play, but you don't need a fourth. Everything goes just as well when there are only three.

You play Old Maid with a regular pack of cards, but before starting, you remove one of the Queens and put her to one side out of the way. This is usually the Queen of Hearts, though some people prefer to take out the Queen of Spades.

Any one of the players can be the first dealer. You do not

have to cut to see who will deal the first hand, as in some other card games. After the first hand is played, the person sitting at the dealer's left deals the next hand, the person at his left the next, and so on around the table.

The dealer gives the player on his left 1 card, then gives each of the other players 1 card at a time, keeping on until all the cards have been dealt. If the cards do not deal out evenly, so that each person has the same number, it doesn't matter.

Each player's object is now to get rid of all his cards as quickly as possible. He does this by forming them into pairs of the same value, such as a pair of Sevens, a pair of Kings, and so on.

After the deal, each player looks at his hand right away. He makes all the pairs he can, and puts them face down in front of him. If he has 4 cards of the same value, such as 4 Tens, he puts them down as 2 pairs. But he is not allowed to put down 3 cards of the same value. He may put down only 2 of them.

When everybody has put down all the pairs he has in his hand, the person at the dealer's left draws a card from the dealer's hand. He can't look at the dealer's cards to choose one that he wants. The dealer keeps the faces of his cards well hidden, and the other player draws without knowing what card he will get.

If the player at the dealer's left draws a card that he can combine with another in his hand to make a pair, he puts the pair face down in front of him. If the new card doesn't help to make a pair, he keeps it and waits for his next turn.

The player at the dealer's left now turns to the person at his left, and that person draws a card from him. After making a pair, if he can, that player lets the player at his left draw a card, and the play goes on in the same way around the table. Each player draws cards from the player on his right. If a player runs out of cards, he is out of the game until the next deal.

The game keeps on until finally only one card is left. This card will always be a Queen, because the Queen with which it could have been combined to make a pair has been removed from the pack.

This Queen is the "Old Maid," and the player who is stuck with her is the "Old Maid"—and the loser.

If you play a number of games one right after the other, this is the usual way to keep score: The first player to get 10 "Old Maids" is the loser, and the player who has had the fewest "Old Maids" is the winner.

It should be added that some people follow the rule that each player draws cards from the person on his left. In this case, the dealer would start the game by drawing a card from the player on his left. This is perfectly all right, as the game is played both ways.

SEVEN-UP or HIGH-LOW-JACK

In some parts of the country, particularly the West, this game is called Seven-Up; and in other parts it is called High-Low-Jack. Whatever it is called, it is a wonderful game. It is usually played by four people, playing as partners, two against two; but it can also be played by two or three.

The game is called Seven-Up because the object is to win a score of 7 points. Its other name, High-Low-Jack, comes from the fact that the highest trump played, the lowest trump played, and the Jack of trumps all count in the scoring.

We will suppose that four people are playing, in partnerships.

The players cut the cards to see who will deal, and the one who cuts the highest card deals. The Ace is the highest card, and the Two the lowest. The dealer gives each player 6 cards, dealing them 3 at a time. He then turns up the next card and puts it on top of the rest of the pack. The suit of this card is trump for the hand that is to be played.

If the turned-up card is a Jack, it counts 1 point for the dealer.

The player at the dealer's left now starts things going, by looking at his cards. The others, including the dealer, leave their cards face-down on the table. If the player on the dealer's left is satisfied with the trump, he says "I start." The others then pick up their cards and the play begins.

A player will decide if he does or does not want the turned-up trump by the cards in his hand. If he has some high cards of the trump card's suit, he will want it to remain trump. But if he is weak in that suit and strong in another suit, he will probably wait to see if he can get a card of his strong suit turned up for trump.

If, therefore, the player on the dealer's left wants another suit for trump, he says, "I beg." The dealer then picks up his hand and looks at it. He can choose to keep the original trump or to change it by turning up another card.

If the dealer wants the original trump, he says, "I give you 1." This is called "gift" and scores 1 point for the player at the dealer's left and his partner.

If the dealer is willing to have another suit as trump, or would rather do this than give a point to the other side, he puts the original trump card on the bottom of the pack. Then he deals 3 more cards to each player, including himself, and turns up the next card for trump. If this card is of the same suit as the first card turned up, he deals 3 more cards to each player and again turns up the next card. This is repeated, if necessary, until a card of a new suit is turned up.

The new suit now definitely becomes trump. The player at the dealer's left is not allowed to "beg" a second time.

The players pick up their cards and, if extra cards have been dealt, they discard the cards they want the least, and keep the 6 cards they think will be most helpful.

The player at the dealer's left leads for the first trick, putting any card he wishes to play face up in the center of the table. If he has the Ace of trumps, he is likely to play it with the hope of capturing the Jack or the Ten. If his partner has either of these high-scoring cards, he will play them on the Ace.

Each player must either follow suit or trump. If he cannot follow suit or play a trump card, he plays any other card. The highest card of the suit led wins the trick, unless a trump card has been played. Then the trump card wins the trick. If more than one trump card is played, the highest one wins the trick.

The winner of each trick picks up the cards, puts them to one side, face down, and leads a card for the next trick.

What each player tries to do in winning tricks is to capture the Jack of trumps, which scores 1 point, and to capture Tens, Aces, Kings, Queens and Jacks. At the end of each deal, these latter cards are added up, according to the following values for them:

A Ten counts 10; an Ace counts 4; a King counts 3; a Queen counts 2; and a Jack counts 1. The person with the highest total wins "game" and scores 1 point.

The various points to be counted are as follows:

High (the highest trump played) counts 1 for the person to whom it is dealt.

Low (the lowest trump played) counts 1 for the person to whom it is dealt.

Jack of trumps counts 1 for the person who wins it in the playing. If the Jack of trumps is also the highest trump played, it is also "High," and scores 2 points.

Jack, if turned up for trump by dealer, counts 1 for the dealer.

Game: The highest total value of cards won in play counts **1** as described above.

Gift: When a player "begs" and the dealer "gives him **1**," it counts 1 for the player who "begs."

Each side adds up its score, and writes it down. The cards are then shuffled, and dealt by the player to the left of the previous dealer. The side that first makes 7 points wins the game.

It sometimes happens that both sides will reach 7 points during the same deal. When this occurs, the points won during that deal are scored in the order of the High, Low, Jack and Game, and the side that wins 7 points first, according to that order, is the winner.

An example or two will make this clear. If one side scores for High and Low, and the other side for Jack and Game, the first side wins, because they won the first two scoring points.

If one side scores for High and Game, and the other side for Low and Jack, the second side wins, for their second point, Jack, comes before Game.

POKER

Poker is one of the most popular of all American card games, and is played by people of all ages in every part of the country. Many have called it the "typical American card game." It is fun because there is a large element of chance and luck in it, and also because good players can bluff about the strength or weakness of their hands and often fool the other players either into making larger bets than they should or else into dropping out of the game.

The two most widely played forms of poker are called Draw Poker and Stud Poker. These are described below. There are also numerous variations of the game. Two of the most popular of these are also described.

Draw Poker

Draw Poker may be played by two or more players, but the best game is when five to seven people are playing. A regular pack of 52 cards is used. The Ace is the highest card, and is followed by the King, Queen, Jack, and so on down to the Two.

The players sit around the table and one of them deals cards around the table face up, one card to each player, until a Jack is turned up. The player who receives the Jack is the dealer for the first hand. After that, the deal passes to the left after each hand has been played.

Before any cards are dealt to begin the first hand, all the players put one or more buttons, toothpicks, pennies or whatever "chips" are being used, in the center of the table. This is called "making the ante." Each player puts on the table the same amount.

The dealer then deals each player 5 cards face down. He deals them one at a time, one to each player in each round, starting with the player at his left. When the deal is finished, each player picks up his hand and judges its value. The things he looks for, in order of their rank as winning combinations of cards, are as follows.

1. *A Royal Flush.* That is—the 5 highest cards of any suit all together in one hand. For example, the Ace, King, Queen, Jack and Ten of Hearts. This is the highest ranking hand.

2. *A Straight Flush.* That is—any of 5 cards of the same suit in sequence, such as the Three, Four, Five, Six and Seven of Clubs. This particular flush is called "Seven High," because the highest card is a Seven. If two or more players have straight flushes, the one whose top card is the highest is the winner. The Ace may be used as the lowest or highest card of a straight flush.

3. *Four of a Kind.* That is—any 4 cards of the same value, such as 4 Threes or 4 Queens.

4. *A Full House.* That is—any 3 cards of the same value together with 2 other cards of the same value, such as 3 Tens and 2 Sevens. If two or more players have a full house, the one who has the highest three of a kind wins, regardless of the ranks of the pairs.

For example, one player has 3 Tens and 2 Kings. Another player has 3 Queens and 2 Fives. The second player is the winner because his 3 Queens are higher than the first player's

3 Tens. The fact that the first player's 2 Kings are higher than the second player's 2 Fives does not enter into the evaluation of the hands.

5. *A Flush.* That is—any 5 cards of the same suit, such as the Two, Four, Seven, Nine and King of Diamonds. The cards do not have to be in sequence. The-flush just mentioned would be described as "King High," because the King is the highest card.

In comparing the value of two flushes, the winner is the player who has the highest card at the top of his flush. If the highest cards are equal in value, the next-highest cards determine the winner. If these are also equal, the third-highest cards are compared, and so on.

6. *A Straight.* That is—any consecutive sequence of 5 cards, not of the same suit. For example, Four of Diamonds, Five of Clubs, Six of Spades, Seven of Diamonds, Eight of Hearts. In comparing the value of two or more straights, the winner is the player who has the highest card. The Ace may be used as either high or low card in a straight.

7. *Three of a Kind.* That is—any 3 cards of the same value together in one hand, such as 3 Twos, 3 Aces or 3 Fives, with 2 other cards that are not a pair of the same value. The winning three of a kind is the one that contains the 3 cards of the highest value.

8. *Two Pairs.* This is any 2 cards of the same value together in the hand with 2 other cards of equal value (but different than the first two), plus 1 odd card. For example, 2 Jacks, 2 Sevens, and a Three. When two or more players have hands containing 2 pairs, the winner is the one who has the highest pair. If the highest pairs are equal, the second-highest pairs are compared. If they are also equal, the odd cards are compared and the player with the highest odd card is the winner.

9. *One Pair.* That is—2 cards of the same value together with 3 cards of differing values. For example, 2 Tens, with an Eight, a Five and a Three. When two or more players have pairs, the winner is the one with the paired cards of the high-

est value. If the pairs are equal, the highest odd cards determine the winner. If these are also equal, the next-highest odd cards are compared, and so on.

10. *High Card.* This is a hand that contains none of the combinations already described. It is valued by the highest card. When two or more players have hands of this kind, the winner is the one who has the highest card. If the highest cards are equal, the next-highest are compared, and so on.

After the players have studied their hands, the game proceeds as follows:

1. The player at the dealer's left has his choice of making the first bet, called "opening the pot." If he does not have a good hand and does not want to bet, he may say, "Check." This means that he wants to stay in the game and may make a bet later on. If he does not want to either bet or check, he says, "I pass." This means that his hand is really poor and he wants to drop out until there is another deal. He then puts his cards face down on the table without showing them to the other players.

2. If the first player does not want to make a bet, the turn goes to the player at his left. He may now make the first bet, or he may check or pass. This procedure continues around the table until one of three things happens: (A) a player makes a bet; (B) all players check; or (C) all the players drop out.

(A) If a player makes a bet, he puts some buttons or chips in the center of the table, adding them to the ante already there. His bet may be small or large. Each player still in the game must now do one of the following things when his turn comes: (1) meet the bet, called "staying" or "calling," which he does by putting chips in the center of the table equal in number to the bet that has been made on this round before it is his turn; or (2) raise the bet, which is done by putting chips on the table equal to the bet, plus some additional chips to make a larger bet; or (3) pass, that is, drop out of the game because he doesn't wish to bet.

No player is permitted to check after a bet has been made.

Also, any player who checked before the opening bet must now meet any bets or raise them, to stay in the game. If a player now drops out of the game, he loses any chips he has put on the table.

In turn, one after the other, the players meet or raise the bet that is on the table when their turn comes. The betting ends when all bets have been met and there are no more raises.

It sometimes happens that a player makes the first bet and all the other players pass. The bettor then wins the pot and the play ends. A deal for a new game follows.

(B) If all the players check, they all qualify for the draw—the drawing of cards that follows the conclusion of the betting, from which draw poker derives its name.

(C) If all the players pass because they have poor hands, there is a new deal. The dealer is the one to the left of the previous dealer. All the chips on the table are left there and are added to the pot of the next game.

After the betting comes the draw. All the players still in the game take part. They discard cards they do not want, and draw new ones from the dealer, hoping they will help to make three of a kind, two pairs, a flush, or some other good combination.

The first player to draw is the one on the dealer's left. He puts the cards he doesn't want to keep face down on the table and tells the dealer: "I'll take two cards," or whatever number it may be to replace the cards discarded.

When there are more than five players, it is customary to limit a player's draw to no more than 3 cards. If there are fewer than five players, each one is usually permitted to draw as many cards as he wishes to. He may even discard his entire hand and draw 5 cards to replace it. It is always best to agree on the number of cards the players may draw, before beginning the game.

If a player has a good hand, he does not have to discard and draw. He "stands pat," and keeps his original hand.

After all players still in the game have drawn, there is a second and final round of betting.

The player who made the opening bet at the beginning of the game once more has his choice of betting, raising the bet, checking, or dropping out of the play. If his new cards obtained in the draw give him a strong hand, he may raise the bet by adding more chips. If his hand is weak, he may wish to drop out.

If the player who made the opening bet is no longer in the game, his turn goes to the next active player on his left.

The second round of betting proceeds in the same way as the first, with each player in turn either checking, meeting the bet, raising the bet, or dropping out of the play.

Before long, all the final bets will have been made. Then comes the big moment—the showdown of all the active players' hands. Each player shows the faces of his cards to the others, and the hand with the highest value wins the pot, or all the chips that are on the table.

In some cases, no showdown is necessary, since some player will already have won. This happens if a player makes a bet that is not met or raised by any other player. The betting player then wins the pot and does not have to show his hand. The play ends, and there is a new deal.

Also, sometimes, only one player will remain in the game, as all the others will have dropped out. In such a case, the one active player wins the pot and is not obliged to show his hand.

If two or more players have hands of equal value at the showdown, they divide the pot equally between them.

After the showdown and the winning of the pot by one of the players, a new hand is dealt by the player at the left of the last dealer, and the game goes on.

Jack Pots

Jack Pots is the most popular variation of straight draw poker, and in many places it has almost taken the place of straight draw poker.

The game starts in the same way as in straight draw poker, with the dealer giving each player 5 cards face down. The player at the dealer's left then has his choice of making the first bet. But, and it is a big but, he may not make a bet unless he has in his hand a pair of Jacks or a combination of cards that rank higher in poker than a pair of Jacks.

If the first player cannot start the betting or does not wish to—even though he has a pair of Jacks or a higher combination—he is permitted to check. The player at his left then has his choice of betting or checking, and so on around the table until some player makes an opening bet.

After that, all the players, including those who have checked, can bet on their hands without regard to the value of their hands. That is, they do not have to have a pair of Jacks or higher. They bet, raise the bet, or drop out of the play just as in straight draw poker.

It sometimes happens that all the players check and no one makes an opening bet. When this occurs, the chips already on the table are left there and new hands are dealt. Also, each player must add more chips to those he has already put down. This is called "sweetening" or "fattening" the pot.

The cards are dealt by the player at the left of the previous dealer, and the player at the new dealer's left has his choice of opening the betting or checking, as described above.

After some player has opened the betting and the other players have met or raised the bet, as in straight draw poker, the players still in the game are entitled to discard cards they do not want and draw others to replace them.

A player may discard any or all of the cards of a combination that entitled him to open the betting and draw new cards to replace them. He must, however, put his discarded cards face down on the table in front of him, so they may be looked at later if necessary.

Cards are drawn just as in straight draw poker and, after the draw, the game goes along exactly as in straight draw poker until the showdown.

At the showdown, the player who made the opening bet in the first round of betting must prove that he had a hand, before the draw, that contained a pair of Jacks or a higher combination. If he cannot prove this, he is not entitled to win the pot.

If no other player met his bet in the first or second round of betting, he will not have drawn any cards and all he has to do is to show the cards that qualified him to open the betting. This proves his case, and he does not need to show his other cards.

If there has been additional betting and a draw, he must show his entire hand.

If the player who made the opening bet in the first round of betting drops out of the play before the showdown, he must have his discarded cards ready, to prove at the showdown that he held a pair of Jacks or higher when he opened the betting.

It sometimes happens that a player opens the betting without having the required high combination of cards. This is done in every case through carelessness or failure to judge the value of the cards correctly. It is not permitted, and no one can open without a pair of Jacks or higher, merely to bluff.

There is a penalty for such a false or illegal opening. Ordinarily, the penalty is to have the player give one chip to all the other players. Another penalty is to have him ante or put up chips for all the other players in the next deal. This is called a "free ride" for the other players.

When it is discovered that a player has opened falsely, he is automatically out of play.

When the discovery is made before the showdown, the other players go right on playing, even though none of them held cards in the beginning high enough to entitle them to open the betting.

When the discovery is made during the showdown, the player with the highest hand wins the pot.

If it is found that a player has opened falsely, after all the other players have dropped out of the play, either before the draw or after it, the pot is left on the table for the next game.

It sometimes happens, after a player has won the pot, that he is found to have opened the betting falsely. When this happens, he cannot be made to return the pot if he has the highest hand. Furthermore, there is no penalty against him. But, to guard against errors, a winner should always be made to show the cards with which he opened the betting, before being allowed to gather in the pot.

Stud Poker

Stud poker differs from draw poker in that, with the exception of one card, all the cards are dealt face up. Each player can, therefore, see most of the other players' cards and can use this information as a guide in making bets. Any number up to ten people can play stud poker.

There is usually no ante before the deal in stud poker. The game starts with the dealer giving each player one card face down, starting with the player at his left. These are called "hole cards." Each player looks at his hole card, but makes sure that nobody else sees it.

The dealer then deals another round of cards, this time face up. These cards are called "up-cards." When the deal is finished, there is a round of betting. The first player to have a chance to bet is the one who has the highest up-card. If two or more players have up-cards of equal value, the player who was first to receive his card has the choice of making the opening bet.

If this player does not want to bet, he may say, "I check." This means that he wants to remain in the game and may want to bet on a later round. Or he may drop out of the play, if his cards do not look good to him. This is called "folding," and a player folds by turning his up-card face down. He does not show his hole card, since it might be one that some other player would like to have.

If the player who has the choice of making the first bet does not want to bet, the turn goes to the player at his left. He may either bet, check or fold. This continues, always going to the left, until (1) some player makes a bet; (2) all the players check; or (3) all the players fold. If all the players fold, there is a new deal.

When some player makes the first bet, he puts one or more chips on the table as his bet. Each player in turn then has the choice of doing one of three things. These are: (1) meeting the bet, called "staying" or "calling," which is done by putting chips on the table equal to those in the first player's bet; (2) raising the bet, which is done by putting chips on the table equal to the first player's bet, plus some additional chips; or (3) folding.

After a bet has been made, no player is permitted to check. Furthermore, any player who checked before the opening bet was made must now meet any bets or raise them, when his turn comes, in order to stay in the game.

When the betting has gone around the table and everyone has had a chance, the players who are still in the game are ready for another round of cards to be dealt. The cards are again dealt face up, and it is customary for the dealer to announce the value of the two cards that are now face up as he puts down the second card. Thus, he will say: "pair of Queens," or whatever they may be. In later deals, when more cards are visible, he not only announces the actual visible combinations, but also the possible ones that the hand may work out to, such as "possible straight," "possible flush," or "possible full house." As a rule, he does not announce any possible combinations lower in value than a straight.

When the second face-up cards have been dealt, there is another round of betting. The player who has the highest card or the highest-ranking combination of cards has the choice of making the first bet. The game goes along as already described until each active player has 5 cards—a hole card and four up-cards. After the fourth up-cards have been dealt, there is a final round of betting. This means that by the time for the showdown there will have been four rounds of betting. This is one of the features that makes stud poker so interesting to play.

Sometimes, only one player is left in the game by the time the showdown arrives. If this happens, he wins the pot and does not have to show his hole card to the others.

After the final round of betting, all the players still in the game turn over their hole cards, so everyone can see them. The hand with the highest value is then the winner of the pot.

Seven-Card Stud Poker

This is a popular variation of straight stud poker. A lot of people like it because it gives the players a better chance to get a good hand. Each player receives 7 cards, instead of only 5, as in straight stud poker.

The dealer first deals a round of cards face down. He immediately repeats, dealing each player a second card face down. Then he deals each player a third card, which is dealt face up.

A round of betting follows, the players basing their bets on their face-up cards. There are then 3 more face-up deals, each followed by a round of betting. Each player now has 2 face-down hole cards and 4 up-cards. A final deal is then made, with the cards dealt face down. This is followed by a final round of betting before the showdown.

At the showdown, each player looks at his 7 cards and chooses the 5 that make the best poker hand. The highest hand wins the pot.

NOTES ON PLAYING POKER

One of the first things a beginning player should do is to become thoroughly familiar with the card combinations, such as the straight, straight flush, full house, and so on. Do this by making up the different combinations and memorizing them, comparing one with another, and making yourself say which is the higher.

One of the great arts in playing poker is bluffing. This is a well-recognized and perfectly legal part of poker-playing. You are allowed to try to mislead the other players as to the strength or weakness of your hand by talking, looking wise, or, if you want to—making believe that you have a weak hand when you really have a strong one—by looking distressed. Don't overdo it, but try to learn to be a good and skillful bluffer. It adds a lot to the fun of the game, and to your chances of winning.

What poker players call "sandbagging" is one well-recognized form of bluffing. When a player who has the choice of opening the betting has a good hand, he often "checks," and stays in the game so he can raise the betting later, after seeing what the other players do and how strong their hands seem to be. This is called "sandbagging."

A variation of this move is for the player to make a very small bet. This may make the others think that he has a poor hand and, at the same time, it lures the other players into the betting, when otherwise they might stay out.

One important basic rule of good poker playing is to drop out of the game as soon as you see you do not have a reasonable chance of winning. This keeps you from betting and saves your chips for the times when you have good hands.

Another important rule is to play your really strong hands for all they are worth. You do not often get a really good hand. When you do get one, judge your chances carefully and bet all you can on them. The winnings they make for you are the important ones.

Last, but not least, never try to force your luck in poker. If you get a run of poor hands, just sit tight and refrain from betting. Sooner or later, you will get a good hand. That is the time to bluff, "sandbag," and do everything you can to raise the bets and build up a big pot that you may be able to win.

12 Games for Large Groups

*The games in this section are all particularly suit-
able for groups of more than four people. They are
games that are fun to play at parties or when the
"gang" is all together and looking for something to
do. They are also first-rate games for mixed groups
of young people and grownups to play.*

*All of these games can be played by smaller num-
bers of players, such as three or four, and some of
them, like Concentration, for example, are often
played by two people. They are classed here as
games for large groups because they are excellent
for that purpose, and because many card games are
not playable by large numbers of people.*

STOP-AND-GO

This game is also called Sequence, and you or some of your
friends may know it by that name. It can be played by any
number up to six.

If there are six players, you deal 8 cards to each, and the
4 remaining cards are called Stops, because they may stop
the play. If five are playing, you deal 9 cards to each, which
leaves you 7 Stops. When four people play, each one is dealt
12 cards, and the 4 cards left over are Stops. If there are three
players, each one is dealt 15 cards, which leaves 7 Stops.

The winner of the game is the first person to play out all
his cards. This is done by playing cards in sequence—5, 6, 7,
8, for example, always following suit, and building up.

Anyone may deal, and the cards are dealt 1 at a time, going

around the table to the left. The second player to deal is the one to the left of the original dealer, and the deal keeps passing on to the left.

The player to the left of the dealer starts the game by playing any card face up in the center of the table, and calling out its value. If it is the Three of Diamonds, for example, he calls out "three."

The next player to the left plays the Four of Diamonds, if he has it. If he does not have it, he loses a chance to play a card. He says "Pass," and the turn goes to the players to the left until someone can play the Four of Diamonds, saying "four."

The needed card, in this case the Four of Diamonds, may of course be one of the Stop cards, which were put to one side. In that case, the sequence will be stopped. Each player will say "Pass." Sometimes quite a few cards of a sequence can be played before it is Stopped.

To make the game "Go" again, the player of the last card plays another card to start a new sequence.

If a player has two or more cards of a sequence in his hand, he plays them, one right after the other, at one time. He does not play one card and then let all the other players say "Pass" before playing the next higher card.

All the cards played are left face up on the table, whether a Stop is reached or whether all the cards of one suit are played out in sequence. No one takes in any cards, since the object of the game is not to take in cards, but to get rid of the cards in your hand.

If a sequence starts with the Three of Diamonds, for example, and the players can build up on it in sequence, the playing keeps on until the King of Diamonds is put out. Then that sequence ends, for a King is always a Stop. You are not allowed to play an Ace on a King to keep a sequence going.

The person who played the King begins a new sequence, playing the Ace of the same suit or any card of any suit.

The best thing to do is to start a sequence with an Ace, for that is the only way to get rid of the Aces. They cannot be played on the Kings, for the Kings are Stops.

SNIP-SNAP-SNORUM

Snip-Snap-Snorum is good for a group of six to eight people, or even more, because it moves fast and keeps everybody busy trying to get rid of his cards. It is so easy to play that it can be learned in a few moments. It is also a good game for smaller groups, and is often played by two people.

There are no formalities about the deal. Anyone can be the dealer. He gives the cards out one at a time, starting with the player on his left. The entire pack is dealt out, and it does not matter if not everyone has exactly the same number of cards.

The object of the game is to get rid of your cards as quickly as possible.

The player at the dealer's left starts the game by putting a card face up in the center of the table and calling out its value. For example, he says "A Six."

The player on his left must then play another Six, if he has one in his hand. If he does not have one, he says "Pass," and the next player to the left takes his turn.

When someone plays the fourth card of a set, such as the fourth Six in the example we are using, he leaves the 4 Sixes in the center of the table, and starts a new set by putting on top of them another card. He calls out its name saying, for example, "A King." The other players who have Kings then play them out as their turns come around.

The winner is the first player who succeeds in getting rid of all of his cards.

It sometimes happens that one player will hold all 3 of the cards that are needed to complete a set of 4 cards. One player, for example, might lead a Ten, and some other player might hold the 3 other Tens. In a case like this, the player with the 3 Tens can put them all on the table at one time, and the hand does not have to be played out in the usual way.

Snip-Snap-Snorum gets its name from the fact that, when it was first played, the person who played the second card of a set of 4 said "Snip," the player of the third card said "Snap," and the player of the fourth card said "Snorum." Lots of people still play this way, and it adds to the fun to call out these zippy words.

GIGGLE

This is a combination card and word game that is a world of fun. The object of the game is to win the greatest number of cards, and it is called Giggle because you can't help laughing at some of the things the players say in their efforts to obey the rules.

It is a good game for a group of five or six, and even seven or eight can play it if there is room for them around the table. If five, six, seven or eight people play, each one is dealt 4 cards, and the rest of the pack is put to one side, as it is not used in the game.

If a smaller number plays, the cards are dealt as follows. For three players, 6 cards to each. For four players, 5 cards to each.

When the cards have been dealt, each player puts his cards face down in front of him.

The dealer starts the game, by starting some sentence, such as, "Bill went for a ride in an airplane. He saw—," or "Dorothy walked down Main Street. She saw—."

After he says the word "saw," he turns the top card of his pile face up and puts it on the table. Then he and the other players try to win the card. This is where the fun comes in.

To win a card, you have to say two adjectives and a noun beginning with the same letter as the value of the card turned face up, and each player tries to be the first to say them.

If an Ace is turned face up, for example, someone could say, "an amiable, affable actress," or "an angular, adorable acrobat." For a Two, a Three or a Ten, you could say, "a tender, tempestuous tangerine," or "a tiny, trembling trout." For a Four or a Five, it would be something like, "a fine, fat funnyman," or "a florid, flip face."

You can see that it takes quite a bit of imagination and quickness to think of things to say, although you can often think of very simple things.

The player who wins a card, by being the first to say three correct words, puts it to one side to keep until the scores are added up. If two or more players say three correct words and finish at exactly the same time, no one wins the card. It is left on the table and belongs to the player who wins the next card.

After the first card has been won, the player on the dealer's left turns up his top card and continues the story by saying, "Bill looked out and saw—," or "Dorothy went on down the street and saw—."

The game goes on, around the table, each player to the left continuing the story. No one may turn a card face up until after saying the word "saw." That is the most important rule. The second is that the cards must be turned face up quickly.

The game ends when all the cards have been won, and the winner is the player who has captured the most cards.

SPADE THE GARDENER

If you don't know the people with the funny names that the cards represent in Spade the Gardener, I hope that you and your friends will make their acquaintance right now. This old English game has been a favorite for many years and Sir Hinkam Funniduster, Sir Hearty John and all the rest of these card people are old friends to many people in both England and America.

Almost any number may play Spade the Gardener, and the more the merrier.

If six people or less play, the game is played with the 20

highest cards—the Ace, King, Queen, Jack and Ten of each suit. Remove these from the pack and shuffle them together.

If more than six people play, use the Nines and Eights also.

Each of the high cards has a special name, and these are as follows:

The King of Spades is Spade the Gardener; the Queen of Spades is Spade the Gardener's Wife; the Jack of Spades is Spade the Gardener's Son; the Ace of Spades is Spade the Gardener's Servant; and the Ten of Spades is Spade the Gardener's Dog.

The King of Diamonds is Sir Hinkam Funniduster; the Queen is Sir Hinkam Funniduster's Wife; the Jack is Sir Hinkam Funniduster's Son; the Ace is Sir Hinkam Funniduster's Servant; and the Ten is Sir Hinkam Funniduster's Dog.

The King of Hearts is Sir Hearty John, and the Queen, Jack, Ace and Ten of Hearts are Sir Hearty John's Wife, Son, Servant and Dog.

The King of Clubs is Club the Constable and the Queen, Jack, Ace and Ten of Clubs are Club the Constable's Wife, Son, Servant and Dog.

The Nines are called cats, the Nine of Spades being Spade the Gardener's Cat, and so on. The Eights are called Canaries.

The game is one in which the players ask one another for cards, and the object is for one player to get all the cards.

Anybody may deal, and the cards are dealt out one at a time to the left around the table. It does not matter if they do not divide evenly among the players.

The player on the dealer's left starts the game by asking any other player for any card. He must always give the card's name. But he does not have to hold a card of a suit to ask for that suit.

For example, Bill, the first player, has no Hearts. But he may ask Mary for Sir Hearty John's Dog, if he wishes to.

Everyone must be extra careful always to use the card's special name. You must never say, for example, "Give me the

Queen of Diamonds." It must always be "Give me Sir Hinkam Funniduster's Wife."

If a player makes a mistake and asks for a card by its usual name, such as the Queen of Diamonds, he must give one of his cards to the player he asked—instead of getting a card himself. The turn then passes to the player from whom he asked the card.

The first player keeps on asking for cards until he asks for a card that another player does not have. Then it is that player's turn. He may begin, if he wishes, by asking the first player for all the cards he has just taken in. He names them one at a time, and the first player must obediently hand them over—even though it hurts.

This is where a good memory comes in handy, and it is one of the things that makes Spade the Gardener different from most other games.

As the game goes on, one player after another will lose all his cards and will have to drop out. The one who finally captures all the cards is the winner.

THE EARL OF COVENTRY

This game, which has been a favorite with young people for many years, is played like Snip-Snap-Snorum, except that instead of saying "Snip," "Snap," and "Snorum," each player says one line of a rhyme.

The first line of the rhyme is made up and spoken by the first player. The second player—the one who matches the first player's card—adds another line, the third player another, and the fourth player adds the fourth and last line. This line *must* contain the words "the Earl of Coventry."

All the lines must be original and made up on the spot. A typical one would be:

First player—"A cat one day went in a wood."

Second player—"She thought that she might find some food."

Third player—"But in the wood was nothing good."

Fourth player—"All she saw was the Earl of Coventry in a hood."

The fourth player always begins the new round by putting down a card and starting a new rhyme. One way to start a rhyme is to mention the card being played, such as, "My card is a heart so red," "Here's a black old Club the Two" or "This time I will play a Queen." You should always try to end the first line with a word that is easy to rhyme.

Take your time about playing the Earl of Coventry. It isn't everybody who can think up a rhyme on the spur of the moment. But you will be surprised what good "Poems" you can sometimes make up.

MY SHIP SAILS

This is a good game for beginners, because it is very easy to play. It is a wonderful game for a group of five or six or even more, and can also be played by three or four people.

Anybody may deal. The dealer gives out the cards one at a time, starting with the player on his left, and gives each player 7 cards. The rest of the pack is put to one side. It is not used in the game.

What each player now tries to do is to be the first to have his cards all of the same suit.

The dealer starts the game by putting one of his cards face down in front of the player at his left. Suppose the dealer has more Hearts than any other suit. He decides to try to get 7 Hearts. He will, therefore, give away a card of some other suit.

The player at the dealer's left now takes a card from his hand and puts it face down in front of the player at his left. Then—and only then—he picks up the card that was given to him by the dealer. If it is a card he wants, that is fine. If not, he plans to give it to his left-hand neighbor on one of his next turns.

The game goes on in this way around the table to the left.

Each player always puts one card face down in front of the player to his left *before* he picks up the card passed to him by the player at his right.

As soon as someone gets 7 cards of the same suit, he calls out, "My ship sails!" He shows the others his hand and is the winner of that game.

An important rule in My Ship Sails is never to tell anyone else what suit you are saving. It often happens that two players try to save the same suit. If they knew about this, one of them would probably switch to another suit—but they don't know. That is part of the fun of this good game.

I DOUBT IT

This is one of the best of all card games for a group larger than four. It can be played by six or eight or as many as can get around the table that is being used; and the more players, the more fun you can get out of the game. The ability to control your expression and to be very convincing, especially when you are in a tight spot, is of the greatest value in playing I Doubt It like an expert.

The object of the game is to be the first player to get rid of all your cards, and this is sometimes quite a task in this topsy-turvy game.

If three or four people are playing, you use a single pack of cards. For six or eight players, however, you should use two packs shuffled together.

The cards are cut to see who will deal, and the person who cuts the highest card is the dealer. In I Doubt It, the King is the highest card and the Ace is the lowest. The deal passes, after each hand played, to the person to the left of the previous dealer.

The dealer distributes the cards one at a time, starting with the player on his left and continuing until all the cards have been dealt out. It does not matter if all the players do not have the same number of cards.

The person at the dealer's left plays first. What he has to do is to put some cards face down on the table. If a single pack is used he puts down from 1 to 4 cards. If a double pack is used he puts down from 1 to 8 cards.

The first player always says that he is putting down Aces. If he puts two cards on the table, for example, he says "Two Aces." He does not have to tell the truth, however, and he is allowed to put down cards other than the Aces if he wishes to.

When the first player has put down his cards, everyone, from left to right around the table, says either "Pass" or "I doubt it."

If someone is suspicious and says "I doubt it," the first player must turn his cards face up.

If the cards are really Aces, the person who said "I doubt it" has to pick them up and add them to the cards in his hand. As the game goes on, the doubter must also pick up any other cards that are on the table. On the other hand, if the cards are not Aces, the first player has to take them back and as the game goes on, any others on the table, and try to get rid of them later.

Sometimes several people will say "I doubt it" all at once.

When this happens, the one who is nearest to the player who put the cards down, according to turn to play, gets the choice.

It is not necessary to doubt every group of cards put on the table. This depends largely on whether the players think someone is trying to get away with something. If no one says "I doubt it," the cards are left face down on the table, and the next player to the left takes his turn.

The player to the left of the first player has to say that he is putting down Twos; the next player Threes; the next one Fours, and so on until the Kings are reached. The next player then starts a new round by saying that he is putting down Aces.

Each player, when his turn comes, must play at least one card. It does not matter if he has none of the cards he is supposed to play. He puts down one or more cards anyway, and even though they are not the right ones, he tries to convince the others that they are. That is where the fun comes in.

Whenever a player has to pick up cards, he has to take all the cards that are on the table.

The winner is the first player to get rid of all his cards. Each of the other players scores 1 point against himself for each card left in his hand. The game usually continues until some player accumulates 300 points against himself. That ends the game, and the player with the lowest score is the winner.

BANGO

With one pack of cards any number of people up to five can have a good time playing Bango. If you have a larger group than five, everybody can get into the game just the same. All you have to do is use two or more packs of cards.

Before the game starts each player is given a number of counters—beans, checkers, toothpicks, or other small objects —and puts one or more of them, according to his wish, into a "pot," or pool. The counters in the pot are placed in the center of the table.

Anybody can deal. Whoever is chosen to be dealer gives each player one card at a time, starting with the player on his left, until everybody has 5 cards. The cards are dealt face up.

The dealer puts the rest of the cards on the table face down in front of him. He starts the game by turning the top card of the pack face up.

Suppose this card is a Five. If some other player has a Five, he calls out, puts the Five on the table, and puts one of his counters on it. He then puts this card, with the counter still resting on it, to one side. Each time the dealer turns up a card, players put a counter on a matching card if they have one.

The dealer takes part in the game, just like the other players. Whenever one of his cards matches a turned-up card, he puts a counter on it and puts it to one side.

The winner is the first player to get a counter on each of the 5 cards that were dealt to him. He calls out "Bango" when this happens, and takes in all the counters in the pot in the center of the table.

The cards are then shuffled and the player to the left of the original dealer deals another hand.

It sometimes happens that no one succeeds in getting a counter on all his cards. When this occurs, the counters in the pot are left on the table for the next hand. Each player, however, always adds one or more counters to the pot at the beginning of each hand.

LOTTERY

Lottery is an old favorite with many and is played by any number of people from five on up to ten or twelve, if that many can get around the table.

Two packs of cards are used, and there are two dealers. These may be chosen by any method the players wish to use. The most popular method is to have the players who cut the 2 highest cards act as dealers.

Before the game starts, each player is given a number of counters, which may be matches, toothpicks, beans, chips or other small objects.

The first dealer gives each player 1 card, *face down*, starting with the person on his left.

As soon as the deal is completed, each player puts an equal number of counters on the table in front of him. Everyone can put out 1 counter, 2 counters or more, as agreed upon; but everyone must use the same number.

The second dealer now gives each player 1 card, which he deals *face up*. The players then turn their first cards face up, and look at everybody else's cards.

If a player's first card (the one dealt face down) matches in value any other player's second card (the one dealt face up), he collects the other player's counters. For example, you turn up your first card and find it is a Two. You find that the second card dealt face up to some other player is a Two. Then you win the other player's counters.

Sometimes two players can match another player's second card. When this happens, the two players divide the counters equally between them.

If a player's first card matches some other player's second card in color (red or black) as well as value, he collects an extra counter from the other player.

If a player's first card matches his own second card in value, he rakes in his own counters, and, if his first card also matches in value some other player's second card, he takes the other player's counters also. In addition, every other player has to give him 1 counter.

When everyone has finished matching cards and collecting counters, the cards are gathered together in separate packs and are dealt out again by the two dealers.

The counters that remain on the table, uncollected, are left there for the next hand around. In addition, however, each player adds an equal number of new counters, just as at the beginning of the game.

If you get to like Lottery and want to play it sometime when there are only three or four people to play, you handle the cards as follows: Use a single pack and divide it into two parts, each containing one red suit and one black suit. One part, for example, might contain all the Hearts and Clubs, and the other part all the Diamonds and Spades. The first dealer deals one part face down, and the second dealer deals the other part face up.

ANIMALS

This game is sometimes called Menagerie, which is a very good name for it, since each of the players calls himself by the name of some animal such as a lion, a tiger, a camel, a giraffe, a rhinoceros or a hippopotamus. Each player announces his animal name before the game starts, and everybody must try his best to remember all the names, for he will need them in playing. This is an especially good game for parties, for any number from three up to eight or even more can play.

The cards are dealt out, face downward, one to each player in turn until the entire pack has been dealt. Each player arranges his cards in a pile, face down, in front of him. It does not matter if the cards come out unevenly so that some players have one more card than others.

The object of the game is to try to win all the cards.

The player at the dealer's left turns the top card of his pile face up and lays it down in front of his pile. He turns the card away from him so that he and all the other players see it at the same time. The other players turn up their cards, one at a time, going around the table from left to right.

They then all turn up their second cards, their third cards and so on. Before long, a player will turn up a card of the same value as the card on top of someone else's face-up pile. When this happens each of the two players tries to be the first to call out the other player's animal name three times in a row. "Cow-cow-cow" or "Bear-bear-bear." The one who finishes calling out the other's name first wins all the face-up cards of his opponent. He takes these cards and places them face down underneath his own face-down pile.

The next play is then made by the losing player, who turns up the top card of his face-down pile.

The game continues in this way until one player has captured all the cards.

If a player turns up all the cards in his pile, he is allowed to turn the pile over and use the cards in it over again. When a player loses all his cards, he drops out of the game until the next deal.

Sometimes a player gets mixed up and calls an opponent by the wrong animal name. If someone does this, he must give the top card of his face-up pile to the player he called by the wrong name.

Then, too, in the general excitement, somebody may call a name by mistake, such as "Tiger-tiger-tiger," when his card does not match any other card on the table. Whoever does this must give his whole face-up pile to the player whose name he called.

One secret of playing Animals is to choose a long name. It will take the other players longer to call it out three times, and give you a better chance of calling out their names first.

CONCENTRATION

Concentration is easy to play, but you have to have a good memory to become an expert. It can be played by any number up to about eight, but you should not overlook the fact that it is also a good game for two or three players.

The dealer, who may be any one of the players, puts the cards one at a time on the table, face down, in no special order, but arranged so that they pretty well cover the table-top.

The idea now is for each player to win as many cards as he can by turning cards face up in pairs of the same value.

The player to the left of the dealer has the first turn, and the play is always in turn to the left.

The first player turns 2 cards face up, one at a time. If they are a pair, such as 2 Aces or 2 Threes, he picks them up and puts them face down in front of him. Then he sees if he can turn up another pair. He keeps on playing until he fails to turn up a pair, which, at the start of the game, is very often.

If a player does not turn up a pair, he puts the 2 cards back on the table, face down, in their original positions. The other players, in turn, then try their luck.

As the game goes on, you will be able to remember the positions and values of some of the cards that have been turned up, if you concentrate. That is why the game is called Concentration. If your memory is good, you will be able to find these cards when you need them to make pairs with other cards you turn face up.

The game ends when all the cards have been made into pairs. Each player then counts his cards, and the one with the most cards is the winner.

MICHIGAN

Michigan, which is sometimes called Michigan Boodle, has been a favorite card game in America for a long time. It is easy to play, and has features that make it different from most other games. If you don't already know it, it is a pretty safe bet that you will enjoy learning and playing it with your friends. It is a good game for a group of six or eight, but may be played by as low a number as three.

A full pack of cards is used, and also 4 cards from a second pack. These cards are the Ace of Hearts, King of Diamonds, Queen of Spades and Jack of Clubs. These cards are called the "boodle" cards. They are placed face up in the center of the table, where they play an important part in the game.

The object of the game is to play cards corresponding to the boodle cards, in order to win counters placed on them. Each player also tries to be the first to get rid of all his cards.

In Michigan, the Ace ranks as the highest card, above the King, and the Two as the lowest. If you cut for the deal, the person cutting the highest card deals first. The deal then goes in turn to the left.

The dealer deals out all the cards in the pack, one at a time. But he deals as though there were an extra player in the game. For example, if six people are playing, he deals 7 hands. The extra hand is at the dealer's left and is the first hand to which he gives a card. If the cards divide unevenly, so that some players have more cards than others, it does not matter.

Before starting to play, each player is given an equal number of counters, such as buttons, beans or toothpicks. Just before each deal each player puts 4 counters on the different boodle cards. He may put one on each card, all 4 on one card, or use any other arrangement.

The dealer starts the game by looking at his cards. If he thinks they are easy ones to get rid of, or if he holds one or more cards that duplicate a boodle card, he will probably decide to keep them. But if he doesn't like his hand, he may exchange it for the extra hand that was dealt.

If he takes the extra hand, he puts his original cards face down on the table, and they are out of the game.

But if he decides to keep his original cards, he must auction off the extra hand to the other players. They have looked at their own cards and can, therefore, decide how much they wish to bid for it. The person who offers the highest number of counters wins the extra hand. He then puts his original cards face down on the table, and they are not used in the game. The dealer takes the counters bid for the extra hand and adds them to his own counters.

This is fair, because everyone gets a turn at being the dealer and can auction off the extra hand if he wants to.

The player at the dealer's left now starts things going by

putting the lowest card of one of the suits in his hand face up in the center of the table and announcing its value, saying "Two," "Three," or "Four." The suit doesn't matter, but he must always play the lowest card of the suit he chooses.

The idea now is to play cards in sequence, building up in one suit. For example, if the first card played is the Two of Hearts, the next card played must be the Three of Hearts, then the Four of Hearts, and so on.

If the first player can play several cards in sequence right away at one time, he does so. But if he cannot do this, the turn goes to the player on his left. If this player cannot play the next higher card in sequence, he says "Pass."

Each sequence is continued until the Ace, as the top card, is played, or until the sequence is stopped because the needed card is in the face-down extra hand. The cards that have been played are left on the table, and the person who played the last card starts a new sequence by playing the lowest card of one of the other suits. For example, if the cards in the first sequence were Hearts, the cards of the second sequence would have to be Clubs, Diamonds or Spades. Each sequence led must be a different suit from the previous one.

If the player has no cards of another suit, the person at his left gets the turn.

As the game goes along, different players will play the duplicates of the boodle cards. When this happens, the player picks up the counters on the corresponding boodle card and adds them to his own.

The game goes on until some player gets rid of all his cards. The other players must then give him one counter for each card they have left in their hands.

If a player runs out of counters, he is out of the game until there is another deal. But some people play so that a player can stay in the game. This is done by each player giving one or more counters to the one who has lost his counters.

Sometimes, at the end of a game, some counters are left on one or more of the boodle cards. This happens when the duplicates of these boodle cards are in the face-down extra hand. These counters are left where they are, so someone can pick them up in the next game.

At the end of a game, the cards are shuffled and dealt out again and each player puts four counters on the boodle cards, just as at the beginning.

The winner is the player who has collected the most counters.

24 Stunts with Cards

♠ ♡ ♣ ◇ ♠ ♡ ♣ ◇ ♠ ♡ ♣ ◇

*These stunts with cards, gathered from far and near,
can give you hours of fun. Some of them are catches,
some are games, and some of them might possibly
be classed as puzzles. All are easy to learn and do,
and I hope you will have a good time with them.*

TOSSING CARDS INTO A HAT

This stunt is like pitching pennies at a wall to see who can
get the most pennies closest to the wall. It is good for hours
of fun, and people can play it over and over again at different
times without getting tired of it.

Open a man's felt hat wide and place it about six feet away
from where you are standing or sitting. If you haven't got
a hat handy, you can use a shoe box or a basket.

Take a pack of playing cards in your hand and try to flip,
throw, or toss the cards into the hat, one at a time. Score 1
for each card that lands in the hat. Let each player go through
the pack and the high man will win. Cards that land on the
brim count as in if they are not knocked off before the end of
the tossing.

There is quite a trick to flicking a card and making it go where you want it to. The best results are usually obtained by holding the cards as shown in the drawing, between the first and second fingers of your right hand. Then curve your wrist back and flip the card on its way with a forward motion of your hand and forearm. If you practice this method, you should be able to get good results and much more accurate direction than by any other means.

MAGNETIZING A CARD

This stunt works best in cold weather, but it usually succeeds in warm weather if you shuffle your feet hard enough. Hold a card in your hand and shuffle your feet along a carpet, moving over toward a wall of the room as you do so. When you reach the wall, slap the card on it and the card will stay there without falling off!

THE FIVE TOUCHING CARDS

Challenge your friends to place 5 cards in such a way that each card will touch each of the 4 other cards.

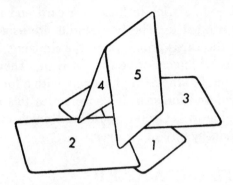

They will undoubtedly fail. You can then proceed to do the stunt by placing the cards as shown in the drawing. It takes a little practice to make the 2 upright cards stand up by leaning them against each other, but it is not really difficult.

AN AMUSING CARD CATCH

Take 5 cards and arrange them as shown in the drawing. Then ask someone if he can take away 2 of the cards, and add 3 cards so that the figure or arrangement of the cards will remain the same.

Better tell your friend that this is a catch, so he will be prepared for what you do. You simply move away the 2 cards at the right and then add the remaining 3 to them.

THE SIX-CARD LIFT

Put 6 cards on the table and then announce that you can lift all 6 of them by picking up one card by the edges while not touching any of the other 5. Make it clear that the stunt is not done simply by pushing one card under the others and then lifting it. When your friends ask how the stunt is done, arrange the cards as shown in the drawing and lift them all by holding the edges of the Ace of Diamonds.

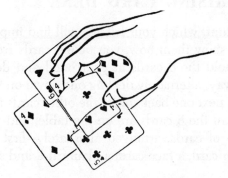

To arrange the cards easily the correct way, first put the card directly under the Ace of Diamonds on the table. Bend the Ace of Diamonds to curve it a little and put it over this card. Put the 2 cards at the right and left over the ends of the Ace of Diamonds. Then put the last 2 cards carefully in place. Each one goes beneath an end of the card under the Ace of Diamonds, but rests on top of the corners of the right- and left-hand cards.

Use old cards if possible, since new ones are so slippery that the cards are likely to slide apart when you lift them.

THE OLD ARMY GAME

This stunt has fooled thousands, and you should have a good time showing it to your friends. Take the 4 Jacks from the pack and put them in a row on the table. Tell your friends they represent four men who decided to enlist in the Army. However, 2 of them, after a physical examination, were rejected while the other 2 were accepted. Ask if anyone can tell which 2 were rejected.

The secret is that on all playing cards made in the United States two of the 4 Jacks have only one eye. These are usually the Jack of Hearts and the Jack of Spades. Very few people notice this, so you can usually baffle your friends.

A SURPRISING CARD DEAL

In this stunt, which your friends will find impossible to do unless you show them how, you take 8 cards from the pack. You then hold the 8 cards in your hand and deal them out in an odd way, alternately dealing one down on the table and putting the next one back *under* the other cards in your hand. Deal until all the 8 cards are on the table, and you wind up with a row of cards, arranged alternately—first a face card, then a plain card, a face card, a plain card, and so on.

The stunt is done by arranging the 8 cards beforehand without letting anyone know. Put 3 plain cards face down on the table. On top of them put 2 face cards, then 1 plain card, then 2 face cards. Put the cards in this order on top of the pack.

When you are ready to show the stunt, take the 8 cards from the top of the pack and lay them helter skelter on the table. Casually pick them up in two's and three's and rearrange them in the right order for dealing, which is the order described above. Tell your friends to watch closely. Then deal the cards as described above.

ONE CARD UNDER THE OTHER

This is a good gag, which always produces a laugh. Put a King and a plain card on the table. The problem is to move the plain card under the King without touching the King. This seems impossible until you take the plain card and hold it under the table directly under the spot where the King is.

THE MASTER AIM

Put a hat on the floor, ask a friend to stand directly over it with a pack of cards in his hand, and try to drop the cards one at a time into the hat. He should drop the cards from about the height of his waist.

Most of the cards will undoubtedly miss the mark and flutter away to the side of the hat as indicated in Fig. 18.

Fig. 18

Fig. 19

You can then show him your master aim by dropping the cards fairly and squarely into the hat. Simply hold them flat, as shown in Fig. 19, and drop them in that position instead of on edge as almost everybody does.

TO MAKE FOUR FIVES EQUAL 16

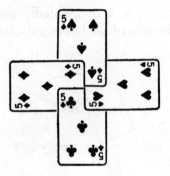

Take the 4 fives from the pack and ask if anyone can lay them out so as to total 16. This seems impossible, but there is a solution and a good one. Simply overlap each card as shown in the drawing and the trick is done.

THE THIRTY-CARD RACE

This is a stunt that you can always win, to the utter bewilderment of your friends who don't know how it is worked. What you do is to deal 30 cards onto the table. Then you and a friend take turns picking up cards. At each turn a player can take any number of cards he wants—from 1 through 6. The winner—who is always yourself—is the one who captures the last notch.

Secret: To win, you must pick up enough cards to be the first to reach these three key numbers: the ninth, the sixteenth and the twenty-third cards. After 23, no matter how many cards your friend takes, he must leave the last one for you.

One way to help you count and always take the right number of cards is to remember that after you reach the first key number, 9, the number of cards your friend takes, plus yours, must always equal 7.

It doesn't matter who is the first to start. If you start, however, always take 2 cards. Then, no matter how many cards your friend takes—from 1 through 6—you can always pick up the ninth card.

THE ONE-TWO-THREE CARD RACE

This is another card race, in which 15 cards are used. You and a friend take turns picking up 1, 2 or 3 cards at each turn. In this race, the idea is *not* to get stuck with the last card. The person who takes the last card is the loser. It is never you.

Secret: Either person can start, although it's easier to win if you do. You will win if after each turn you leave 13, 9 or 5 cards on the table.

If you start, take 2 cards, leaving 13. If your friend starts and you miss out on 13 and 9, catch up on your third turn and leave 5 cards on the table.

MAKING A CARD INVISIBLE

Take a card from the pack and tell one of your friends that you can bewitch him in such a way that the card will be invisible to him, even though the other people in the room will be able to see it.

When you are told that this seems unlikely or even impossible, put the card on top of your friend's head.

STANDING A CARD ON EDGE

Take a card from the pack and ask some friend if he thinks he can stand it upright on one edge. Your friend will probably try, but will find that it just can't be done.

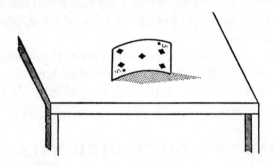

You then proceed to do the stunt by simply bending the card to make it curved, as in the drawing.

THE WHISPERING QUEEN

This is a stunt that is done by two people who are in "cahoots" with each other—that is, they know the secret, but nobody else does. You and a friend do it together at a party or some other gathering.

He is to stay in the room while you go into the next room. When you are gone, he holds up the Queen of Hearts facing someone, so the Queen can have a good, close look. He then tells you to come in, and gives you the Queen. You hold the card close to your ear so it can whisper the name of the person it looked at, and then you name the person. Everyone is pretty surprised, but the principle is very simple.

Your friend signals the right person to you by sitting or standing in the same position. If the person is sitting up straight with hands folded, your friend does the same. If the person has his legs crossed, your friend crosses his, and so on. After a little practice, two people can usually master this stunt so that it never fails.

YOU CAN'T LOSE

Give a friend a pack of cards and ask him to remove a number of them, and count them secretly to see if he has an odd or even number of cards. When this is done, take a few cards from the pack yourself. Then tell your friend that when your cards are added to his, the total number of cards will be an even number, if he has an odd number of cards, or an odd number, if he is holding an even number of cards.

You can't lose. You always take an *odd* number of cards— 3, for example—from the pack. If these are added to an odd number such as 5, the total will be an even number, 8. If they are added to an even number, such as 4, the total will be an odd number, 7.

COIN ON CARD STUNT

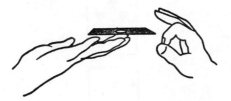

If you can get several friends all trying to do this stunt at once you can have a barrel of fun. Balance a card on the second finger of your left hand. Then take a coin and place it on top of the card directly over the tip of your second finger, as in the drawing. The stunt is to remove the card without touching or dropping the coin.

It all depends on how deft you are. Just flick the card with the first or second finger of the right hand, striking it right at the end of one of the corners. The card will fly away in a whirling motion and, if you are good, the coin will drop directly on the second finger of the left hand.

CARD CROSS STUNT

It's surprising how many people you can puzzle with this stunt. Most people will believe it isn't possible until you show them how to do it.

Arrange 6 cards in the form of a cross, as shown in the drawing. Then ask a friend if he can move 1 card to make the cross have 4 cards in each crosspiece.

The stunt is done by picking up the bottom card of the vertical row and putting it on top of the second card from the top. Each crosspiece will then contain 4 cards, though not in the way your friend may have expected.

ALL IN ORDER

In doing this card-dealing stunt, you take 13 cards from the top of the pack and deal them as follows:

Hold the 13 cards in your hand, face down. The rest of the pack is not used. Put the top card in your hand, under the 12 others, face down. Put the next card on the table, face up. Put the next one under the order cards, the next one on the table, and so on until all 13 cards are on the table. The surprising thing is that the cards are in numbered order, and run in sequence from the Ace up to the King!

To do the stunt, arrange the cards beforehand. Put the Ten face down on the table. On top of it put, face down, the Six, King, Five, Nine, Four, Jack, Three, Eight, Two, Queen, Ace and Seven. Keep the cards in this order and put them face down on top of the pack.

When you are ready to begin, remove these pre-arranged 13 cards and deal them as described above. The effect is quite uncanny as, one after the other, the cards come out in numerical order.

If your friends think the stunt is easy to do, give them the thirteen cards and let them try it!

A BAFFLING CARD STUNT

This stunt has always been a favorite of mine; I have used it many times and had a lot of fun with it. Few people ever catch on to it.

Ask a friend to take any number of cards up to 15 from a pack, to count the cards, but not to let you know how many he has. You then take some cards, always being sure to take more than 20. Just count your cards off silently. We will assume that you took 23 and that your friend took 14 cards, although you do not know or need to know the number he has.

Now you say, "I have as many cards as you have, and enough more to make 19 and 4 over." Both of you start counting your cards onto the table. When he reaches 14, he will put down his last card. Then you repeat, "I said I had enough more to make 19—that means 5—" and you count 1, 2, 3, 4, 5 cards onto the table, "and 4 cards left over," and you show the 4 cards in your hand.

The explanation of this is simplicity itself. All you do is to say that you have 23 cards, but you say it in such a way that everybody is mystified. When you say that you have enough more cards to make 19 and 4 over, you are saying that you have 19 plus 4 cards, or 23 cards. You could also say "I have enough more to make 18 and 5 over," or "to make 17 and 6 over," always starting with some number over 15, which is the most your friend can have.

Try it out with a friend and you will see how baffling a stunt it is.

WHAT'S ON YOUR MIND?

This stunt is always good for a laugh, especially if you show it to some friend when there are other members of your gang present.

You deal 6 cards face down from the top of the pack, dealing 1 to your friend, 1 to yourself, 1 to your friend, 1 to yourself, and so on until you each have 3 cards. Then you ask your friend, "What's on your mind?" It doesn't matter what he replies. You tell him that you are sure you know what is really on his mind and that you have dealt him cards that reveal the secret. He turns up the cards, and they are 3 Queens!

You pick the cards up and say, "Well, let's try it again. Maybe it will come out different!" But, each time your friend gets 3 Queens, and you can keep it up as long as you like, dealing him 3 Queens time after time.

To arrange the cards for this stunt, you take the 4 Queens and put them face down on top of the pack with 1 ordinary card among them. From the top down, the cards should be arranged in this order: 3 Queens, the ordinary card, then the fourth Queen. The sixth card will be the next card on the pack—it doesn't matter what it is.

Now take the pack face down in your left hand, deal the top card face down to your friend, the next one face down to yourself, and so on. He will have 3 Queens. While he is looking at them, slip the top card of your 3 face-down cards to the bottom, beneath the other 2. Put your 3 face-down cards on the pack, then put your friend's 3 Queens face down on top of them. Then deal again and he will once more get 3 Queens.

You can continue to deal as long as you like, with the same result, by always putting your top face-down card under your two other face-down cards, and putting your friend's Queens on top of them.

THE ELEVENS STUNT

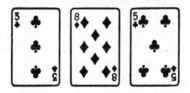

Tell your friends that you can put 3 cards on the table as often as you wish to form numbers that can be divided evenly by 11 without leaving any remainder. Then challenge them to see if they can figure out how you do it.

The drawing shows an example—a Three, an Eight and a Five, forming the number 3 8 5. Divide 11 into 385 and it goes 35 times exactly. You can do this over and over with different groups of cards, and your friends will have a mighty hard time guessing the secret.

The secret is always to have the values of the first and third cards add up to the value of the middle card. Thus, in the drawing, the Three and the Five add up to Eight.

BUILDING CARD CASTLES

Building card castles takes steady hands and a good deal of patience. But the results are worth it, if you are successful. You can build castles four, five or even six stories high if you can balance the cards accurately and steadily.

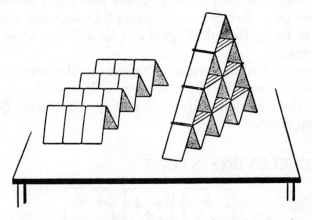

If you have never tried to make a card castle, the drawing will show you what one looks like. They are made by resting pairs of cards against each other at an angle.

The first story may consist of a single row of three or more pairs of cards. When these are in place, you lay a floor of cards on top of them. Then you build a second story by balancing more cards together on the floor and, if you can, you go on to add additional stories until you have room for only one pair of cards at the top of the castle.

Very often, of course, some pair of cards will give way, and the whole building will come tumbling down before it is completed. Then you just pick up the cards and start all over again from the beginning.

When you get really good at building with cards, try making a first story of three or four rows, each row containing three or four pairs of balanced cards. Roof this over with cards, laid flat to form an oblong or square platform, and go on building on top of it.

SPELLING BEE

Here is another dealing-out stunt that is first rate: Hold 13 cards in your hand and deal them, spelling out the numbers of the cards, 1 card for each letter. At the end, all 13 cards lie beside each other on the table, arranged in proper numerical order or sequence.

Begin by spelling A-C-E, and as you say each letter, put the top card at the bottom of the packet of 13 face-down cards in your hand. Then put the next card face up on the table. It's an Ace.

Then spell T-W-O, putting a card under the packet for each letter, and then put the next card face up on the table. It's a Two. Keep on in the same way, spelling out T-H-R-E-E and putting the next card on the table and so on right up through the Jack and Queen. Then the King is the only card left in your hand, and you place it on the table.

At the end, all 13 cards lie beside each other, arranged in proper numerical order or sequence.

To do this stunt, the 13 cards of one suit are arranged as follows: Put the Five face down on the table. On top of it put face down the Nine, Ten, King, Jack, Two, Four, Six, Queen, Ace, Seven, Eight and Three.

Then deal as described above, and you can't miss.

17 Magic Tricks with Cards

♠ ♡ ♣ ◇ ♠ ♡ ♣ ◇ ♠ ♡ ♣ ◇

This section contains seventeen of the best magic card tricks that have dramatic effects and that are easy to do. None of them requires sleight of hand. All of them are good. If you learn some of them and practice them well, you should be able to acquire a real reputation as a wizard. For the best results, do not give away the secrets of how the tricks are done.

TELLING A CHOSEN CARD

Ask someone to draw a card from the pack and look at it without showing it to anyone else. Ask him to multiply the value of the card (the number, if it is a plain card, of its spots) by 3, add 6 to the product, then divide the last answer by 3. Tell him to give you the result. Then subtract 2 from that number and you will be able to tell him the value of his card.

The Aces count as 1, Jacks count as 11, the Queens as 12, and the Kings as 13.

Example. Supposing your friend drew a Ten. He multiplies it by 3 and gets 30. He adds 6 and gets 36. He divides this by 3 and gets 12, which is the number he tells you. You subtract 2 from 12 and say:

"Your card is a Ten!"

THE REVERSED CARD

This trick is a very mystifying one, although the key to the mystery is always right before the eyes of the people to whom you show it. To do it, put 5 or 6 cards on the table in a row, as in the drawing. Then turn your back to the cards and ask someone to turn upside down any card he pleases—not face-down but simply around so the top and bottom ends change places. He does so and you turn to the cards, concentrate for a moment, and point out which card has been reversed or turned around.

The trick is done by using cards that magicians call "pointers." In every pack there are a number of cards that have more spots pointing in one direction than in the other. The drawing above shows a few of these "pointers." There are others that you can easily find by looking through the pack.

Before you do the trick you select some of these cards and put them on top of the pack, making sure that all point in the same direction. Lay them out, without turning them, and notice which way they all point. Then, when someone reverses a card, you can easily discover it.

You can also use the "pointer" cards to tell what card a person draws from the pack. Arrange a pack containing only the pointers, and have them all pointing one way. After someone draws a card, reverse the pack, and have the card put back in it. Then deal the cards out face up on the table. The card which is pointing the wrong way is the chosen one.

CUT THE PACK

This method of telling a chosen card has been used by many professional magicians and is well worth learning. It is mystifying and it requires absolutely no sleight of hand.

Shuffle a pack of cards thoroughly and just as you finish, glance at the top card. If this seems hard to do without being detected, just hold the pack face up in one hand and run the cards over into your other hand as though looking casually through the pack. While you are doing this, it is easy to see and memorize the top card.

Give the pack to someone and ask him to put it face down on the table and cut it into two piles. Pick up the pile that formed the bottom part of the pack and put it on the rest of the cards at right angles as in the drawing.

Now talk for a moment, saying that the pack was cut wherever the spectator wished and that you, of course, have no way of knowing what card it was cut at. This is simply to let a moment or two go by so the spectators will forget which was the top and which the bottom part of the pack.

Ask someone to pick up the top half and to look at the top card of the bottom half. This is the card you know. It was the top card of the pack at the start. Now you know the "chosen" card and can name it right away.

THE LIE-DETECTOR TRICK

Tell your friends that you have developed to an uncanny degree your ability to tell whether or not a person is telling the truth. This came about, you might add, after many long years of study in the Orient. Be that as it may, this is a good card trick, and this is how it is done.

As you shuffle the cards or hold them in your hands, look at and remember the fourth card from the top of the pack. Let's say it is the Three of Hearts. Now cut the pack into 3 piles on the table. Take 4 cards off the pile that was on top of the pack. Deal out a card on top of each of the 3 piles and give the fourth card to a spectator. This is the Three of Hearts, but no one knows that you know it.

Now have the spectator replace the card in any one of the piles, put the piles together, and shuffle the cards as much as he wants to. Then ask him to deal out the cards face up one at a time, while he says "Yes" or "No" for each card. His idea is to make it impossible for you to tell if he is naming the chosen card. You don't care, however, for when you see the Three of Hearts you say it is the chosen card, even though the dealer may have said "No." Nothing can beat that old Oriental lie-detecting system.

INSTANTANEOUS REVERSAL

This is a trick that will make your friends think you are a master of sleight of hand. It really works itself.

Before you start, put the Seven of *Clubs* and the Eight of *Spades* in the pack reversed so that they are face up, as shown in the drawing. When starting the trick, run through the cards and pick out the Seven of *Spades* and the Eight of *Clubs*.

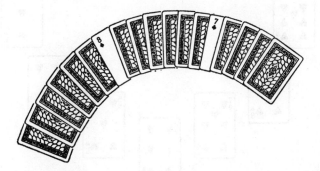

Hold these up and say, "Now watch me closely. The hand is quicker than the eye." You say this to avoid saying, "Here is the Seven of Spades and the Eight of Clubs." Just let the spectators look at the cards. Then proceed.

Put the 2 cards face down into the face-down pack. Snap your fingers at the pack and spread it out face down. The spectators will see the two other cards face up and because the cards are so alike they will think that you have turned them over by sleight of hand.

MYSTIC TAPPIT

Arrange 12 cards running from an Ace to a Queen in the form of a clock dial, as shown in the drawing. Then ask someone to think of one of the cards but not to tell you which one it is.

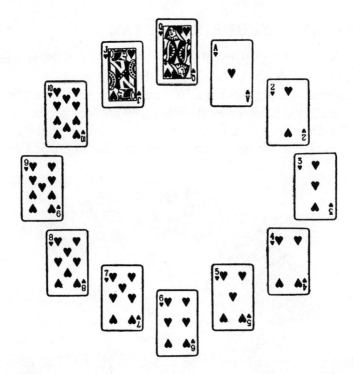

Now tell your friend that as you tap your pencil on the cards he is to count the taps silently, but is to begin with the number next higher than the card he chose and count up from there. For example, if he selected a Five, he would count your first tap as 6, your second tap as 7, and so on. Tell him to say "Stop" when his count reaches 20, and that you will tell him which card he secretly selected.

Secret: First tap the Seven, then the Six, then the Five, and so on around the circle of cards. If you do this, your pencil will always be tapping the chosen card when your friend says "Stop."

SURE WAY TO FIND A CHOSEN CARD

Every amateur magician should know this professional secret. With it you can let a person draw any card from a pack and you can always find the card.

The secret is this. Simply look at and remember the bottom card of the pack. Have a person take a card, look at it, and replace it on the top of the pack. Then cut the cards, putting the bottom half on top; this puts the bottom card, which you know, directly on top of the chosen card. The cards can then be cut many times, but whenever you want to reveal the chosen card, it will be waiting for you directly below the card that was originally the bottom card.

FOUR-ACE PRODUCTION

You can perform the small miracle of producing the 4 Aces from the pack after it has been shuffled and placed in your coat pocket, if you follow the method given here.

Before doing the trick, secretly remove the 4 Aces from the pack and put them in your right-hand coat pocket. Then let anyone shuffle the pack thoroughly. Take the pack and put it in your pocket, putting it outside of the Aces.

Tell the spectators that your little finger is extraordinarily sensitive and can tell an Ace immediately by touch. Then reach into your pocket and bring out the Aces one at a time.

THE THREE FRIENDLY QUEENS

Take 3 of the Queens from a pack and hand them to a friend. Ask him to put them back in the face-down pack, one on the top, one in the middle, and one on the bottom. He is then to cut the pack several times, putting the bottom half on the top half. Despite this mixing-up, the Queens are such friends that when you run through the pack face up, they are found together.

Secret: As you look for the 3 Queens at the beginning of the trick, slip the fourth Queen on the bottom of the pack. Then, when the cards are cut, 3 Queens will be brought together. The sharpest eyes fail to notice the change in the suit of one of the Queens—that one being the fourth Queen secretly placed on the bottom of the pack.

THE THREE-CARD ANSWER

Ask a friend to take from the pack 3 cards that are in successive order, such as Two, Three and Four, or Six, Seven and Eight. When he has done this, ask him to arrange them

in a row, without your seeing them, so that the highest card is on the left, the next highest in the middle and the lowest on the right, as in the drawing.

Suppose he picks a Six, a Seven and an Eight. He puts them in a row, which makes the number 876. Ask him to reverse their order in his mind and to subtract the number they then make from the number they made in the original order. He does this and subtracts 678 from 876, using pencil and paper.

You then look through the pack and remove 3 cards. "Is this the answer?" you ask, holding up the 3 cards. Yes, it is the answer, and you always guess it correctly.

Here's how it's done. The answer will always be 198. All you have to do is remove an Ace, a Nine and an Eight, arrange them in order, and the trick is done.

A FAMOUS FOUR-ACE TRICK

This is a simple and easily done card mystery, but a very baffling one.

Take the 4 Aces from the pack and give them to someone to hold. You then ask him to put 1 Ace on top of the pack, 1 on the bottom, and the remaining 2 in the middle. You then cut the pack several times and spread out the cards or deal them onto the table. All 4 Aces are found together!

TOP HALF BOTTOM HALF

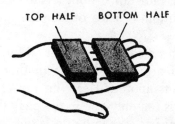

The trick is done as follows. As soon as the first 2 Aces have been put on the top and bottom, put the pack on the palm of your left hand and cut it into halves, as shown in the drawing. Immediately pick up the bottom half with your right

hand. Then ask your friend to put the remaining 2 Aces on top of the top half. When he has done this, put the bottom half on top of the rest of the cards, and the 4 Aces will all be together. You can then cut the pack as often as you wish and the Aces will not be separated.

THE GREAT "STOP!" TRICK

This trick is a stunner! Be sure to learn it. You give a pack of cards to a friend and ask him to deal onto the table 6 piles face down in a row, adding 1 card to each pile on each round of dealing from left to right. He is then to take a card from the middle of any pile, look at it, replace it face down on top of the pile, then put the rest of the piles on top, and cut the cards several times.

You then ask him to deal out the cards one at a time, naming each card. When he comes to his chosen card you say, "Stop! You just dealt your card." And it always is. The great part of this trick is that you never touch or go near the cards from start to finish, which makes it seem impossible to do.

Secret: This is really clever. Before doing the trick, remove 4 Sevens or any other 4 cards of the same value from the pack, so 48 cards remain, 12 in each suit. Then put 6 cards of one suit—Hearts, for example—on top of the pack, and 6 more Hearts on the bottom. Thus, when your friend deals the cards out into 6 piles, face down from left to right, there will be a Heart at the bottom of each of his piles and a Heart on the top.

When he takes a card and puts it on top of a pile, he puts it on top of a Heart. When he puts another pile on top of the first one, he puts another Heart on top of his chosen card. Thus, his card is the only one in the pack that is sandwiched in between 2 Hearts. When he deals out the cards and says, for example, "Three of Hearts, Eight of Clubs, Nine of Hearts," you will know that his card must be the Eight of Clubs.

MAGIC CARD REVELATION

Give someone a pack of cards and ask him to pick a card and hold it up so that everybody, including yourself, can see it. You then take back the pack, put it in your coat pocket, and say, "Now watch this closely. I am going to draw out cards from the pack that will match the chosen card. The trick is done by my educated little finger."

Suppose the chosen card is the Nine of Hearts. You reach into your pocket and bring out an Eight and an Ace which, added together make 9. Then you reach in again and bring out a Heart to match the suit of the chosen card.

How do you do it? Well, here's the secret. Before starting the trick you put 4 special cards in your pocket. These are the Ace of Diamonds, Two of Spades, Four of Hearts and Eight of Clubs. With these 4 cards you can match the number and the suit of any card in the pack. Try it and you'll see how it works. But be sure that you remember the order of the special cards in your pocket so that you can always bring out the one you want.

INSTANT CARD LOCATION

Sometimes the simpler a card trick is, the more it fools your friends. This is a trick of that kind. You take a pack of cards and cut it into halves. Then you have someone choose 2 cards from one heap, look at them, and put them into the other half of the pack. Ask him to shuffle thoroughly the half into which he has put the cards. You take the half from him after the shuffling and immediately pick out the cards he selected.

The secret of this trick lies in the fact that you have separated the cards beforehand. In one half you have put all the even cards like Two, Four, Six, Eight, Ten and Queen. All the others go into the "odd" half—all odd numbers like Ace (1), Three, Five, Seven and so on. Then all you need to do to discover the chosen cards is to look at the half of the pack into which they were put. If it is the "odd" half, the chosen cards will be the only even ones in it, and vice versa.

To make it easy to cut the pack into the two halves, curve the upper half a little as shown in the drawing.

HIT THE DECK

Ask someone to choose a card, memorize it and replace it on top of the pack without your seeing what the card is. You then cut the cards, putting as usual, the bottom part of the pack on the top part, and tell your friend that to make the trick work you want him to "hit the deck." (Deck is another word used for a pack of playing cards.) Hold the cards in your hands and have him hit them several times.

Then spread out the cards face down. The hitting has apparently reversed one card, for there is a card face upward in the pack. "Aha," you say, "the trick has worked," and you immediately draw out the chosen card from the face-down pack.

The preparation for this trick before it is shown is turning face up the fifth card from the bottom of the pack. Then, when your friend takes a card, replaces it on the top of the pack, and the pack is cut, the chosen card will be the fifth card beneath the face-up card. Having your friend "hit the deck" is just a bit of diversion to make it harder to guess how the trick is done.

THE MAHATMA MARVEL CARD TRICK

This trick is so impossible to detect that it is named for the mahatmas or master magicians of the Orient. Yet it is so easy to do that you can learn it in a few moments.

You give a well-shuffled pack of cards to a friend and ask him to count down from the top any number between 1 and 10 and remember the card at that number. He is also to remember the number of cards it is from the top—the third, fourth, fifth or some other number. He is then to cut the cards so that nobody will know the location of the secretly chosen card.

Next you ask your friend to deal the cards on the table from left to right in the same number of piles as the number of cards his chosen card was from the top, adding 1 card to each pile on each round of dealing. For example, if he chose the third card from the top he would deal the cards out into 3 piles. If his card was the fifth from the top, he would deal the cards into 5 piles, and so on.

When this has been done, ask your friend to pick up the piles—in any order—and to give them all to you. Then, by simply looking through the cards, you can immediately find the chosen one.

All you have to do is to look at and remember the bottom card of the pack at the start of the trick. Then proceed just as described above. When your friend deals the cards onto the table in the same number of piles as the number his card was from the top, he automatically causes the bottom card and the chosen card to come together. It's hard to believe but it's true.

When you look through the cards held face up and spread out from left to right in your hand, the card just to the right of the original bottom card will be the chosen card.

MIRACLE SPOT REVELATION

This is not "just another trick." It is a card trick known to professional magicians and used by them. Its effect is dramatic and it requires no sleight of hand. I have done it hundreds of times and I would urge you to learn it because you will enjoy doing it.

The effect is, briefly, that you deal a pack of cards face down into a number of piles on the table. You ask someone to choose 3 of the piles. This is done, and you then ask your friend to turn 2 of the 3 piles face up. The third pile is left face down, but you immediately name the number of spots on its bottom card. The pile is turned face up—and you are always right!

This is how you do it: Take the pack of cards in your hand. Lift off the top card and show it. Suppose it is a Six. Put it on the table, face down. Then begin to count from the number of the card—in this case, six. Put a card from the pack on the first card, face down, and say "Seven." Continue this until you have counted to ten. This makes a pile of 5 cards.

Now turn up the next card of the pack and do the same thing, starting to count from whatever its number may be. Put this card face down, beside the first pile, and count up to ten as before, adding a card for each number counted.

Repeat this process of counting to ten from whatever number the turned-up card is until you have no more cards in your hand.

The face cards—King, Queen and Jack—and also the Tens, are put by themselves in one pile. If you turn up one of these cards, put it aside by itself. Then, if you turn up others, put them on top, all in the same pile.

When all the piles are completed, pick up all that contain

less than 4 cards. Also pick up the last pile you dealt out, unless it came out even on the count of ten. Even though it may contain more than 4 cards, pick up this pile, unless it made an even ten. Put the piles you pick up to one side, and on top of the face cards and Tens you have put to one side.

Now ask your friend to select 3 of the piles. When he has done this, ask him to pick up all the other piles and give them to you. Take these cards and add them to the cards you have piled together. This leaves only the 3 chosen piles on the table.

Run the cards of the pile you have put to one side from one hand to the other, and count off silently 19 cards. Put these down. Then ask your friend to turn over 2 of the 3 chosen piles. Assume that the bottom cards are a Three and a Four, as in the drawing. Add these together to get 7. Then remove 7 cards from those remaining in your hand.

The number of cards left in your hand will now tell you the number of spots on the bottom card of the third chosen pile. If you have 3 cards left, the card is a Three, and so on. Announce the number of spots. Then turn the pile over and reveal the hidden card.

This trick works on a mathematical principle and will always succeed if you do each move properly.

25 Puzzles with Cards

♠ ♡ ♣ ◇ ♠ ♡ ♣ ◇ ♠ ♡ ♣ ◇

(See answers on page 168.)

CHANGING THE ROWS

Take 8 face cards from the pack, and 8 of the lower cards such as Threes, Fours and Fives. Then arrange them in 4 rows on a table, alternately, 4 in a row, as shown in the drawing (Fig. 20).

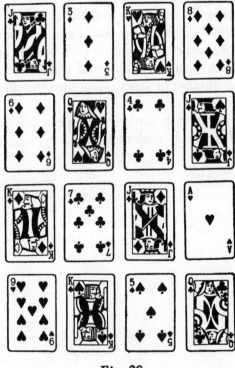

Fig. 20

[150]

The puzzle now is to move 2 cards to different positions so that every card can be in a row consisting entirely of face cards or entirely of lower cards. The first or left-hand row will be all face cards, the second row all lower cards, the third row all face cards, and so on.

There is a little catch to this, so be prepared for it. The rows in the solution don't necessarily have to be straight up-and-down and across.

THE ADD-TO-18 PUZZLE

This is one of the puzzles that you can figure out without too much difficulty if you work at it a bit.

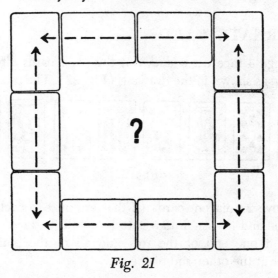

Fig. 21

The puzzle is to take 10 cards from a pack, beginning with an Ace and up to and including a Ten, and then see if you can arrange them in a hollow square like the one shown in the drawing (Fig. 21) so that the spots on the cards forming the four sides add up to 18 for each one of the 4 sides. The spots on 4 cards are to be added together in the top and bottom rows, and the spots on 3 cards in the side rows.

THREE-IN-A-ROW

Put 3 cards—any cards will do—in a row on the table. Then see if you can remove the middle card from its central position without touching it.

THE SIXTEEN-CARD PUZZLE

Take all the Kings, Queens, Jacks and Aces from a pack of cards—16 cards all told. Then see if you can arrange the 16 cards in 4 rows of 4 cards each, so that no 2 of the same suit or of the same value are in any one 4-card row—up and down, straight across, or diagonal.

ALTERNATE CARDS

Arrange 4 face cards and 4 of the plain cards alternately in a row, as shown in the drawing (Fig. 22). The puzzle then

Fig. 22

is to move 2 adjacent cards (2 that are next to each other) at a time and in 4 such moves to bring all the face cards together at one end of the row and all of the plain cards together at the other end of the row.

THE FIVE-KINGS PUZZLE

Put any 10 cards in a row face down on the table, as shown in the drawing (Fig. 23). What you must then try to do is to pick up a card, jump it over 2 cards next to it—to left or right—and make a king of the next or third card—a king being 2 cards, one on top of the other, as in checkers.

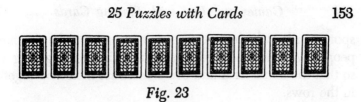

Fig. 23

Then you must keep on jumping over 2 cards at a time in the same way until all the cards are arranged 2 together as kings. When you jump over a king, you are to consider it as 2 cards. You can jump both to the right and the left, and there are 5 jumps in all.

THE NOBLE LORDS AND THE COMMONERS

Take from the pack 6 face cards, which we are here calling the "noble lords"; and at the same time remove 6 plain (or

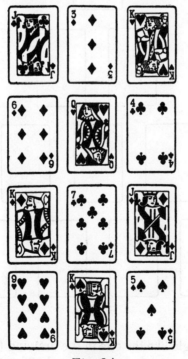

Fig. 24

spot) cards, which in this puzzle represent the "common people." Arrange the cards as shown in the drawing (Fig. 24) so that the noble lords and commoners are mixed up together in the rows.

Now, by touching only 1 card, see if you can make the top row and the third row from the top all noblemen, and the second and fourth rows all commoners. There is a little catch to this, so see if you can find it out.

TRICKY TRIANGLE

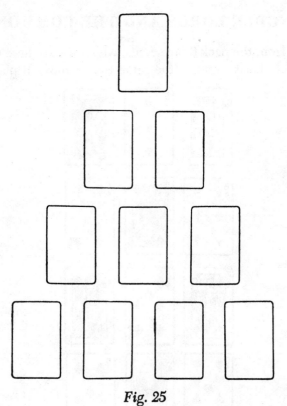

Fig. 25

Make a triangle like the one in the drawing (Fig. 25) using any 10 face-down cards from the pack. Then see if you can turn the triangle upside down—so that it is pointing down instead of up—by moving 3 of the cards.

FACE-UP

Put 3 cards on the table in a row. The 2 end cards are turned face down, and the center card is face up (Fig. 26).

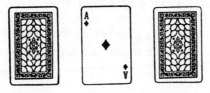

Fig. 26

The puzzle now is to make 3 moves, turning over 2 cards at each move, and finish with all 3 cards face up.

THE STAR PUZZLE

Take any 10 cards from the pack and put them in a heap on the table. Then see if you can arrange them to form a star, made up of 5 lines or rows of 4 cards each.

THE JEALOUS KINGS

Take from the pack the King and Queen of Clubs, the King and Queen of Hearts, and the King and Queen of Diamonds. These represent three happily married couples; but the Kings, or husbands, are all very jealous men.

One day they all went out walking together and came to a river. There was only one boat in which they could get across, and it would hold only two people at a time. The Kings said that no King could be with a Queen unless her husband (the King of the same suit) was present, either on land or in the boat.

How, under these circumstances, did they cross the river in the boat?

Take the 6 cards and see if you can move them across an imaginary river on your table, so that no Queen is ever with a King of another suit unless the King of her own suit is with her.

THE HOURGLASS PUZZLE

Take cards with spots numbering from 1 (an Ace) up to 7 from the pack. Then see if you can arrange them in the hour-

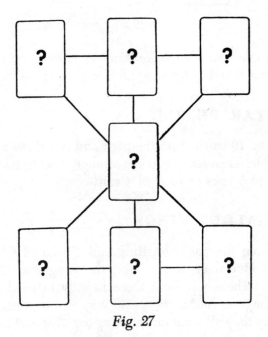

Fig. 27

glass pattern shown in the drawing (Fig. 27) so that the spots on the cards in each 3-card row—straight across, up and down, and diagonal—add up to 12.

THE EIGHTEEN-CARD CIRCLE

This is a good deal like the Hourglass Puzzle, but is harder. You need 11 cards, ranging from an Ace up to a Jack. The value of the Jack is 11.

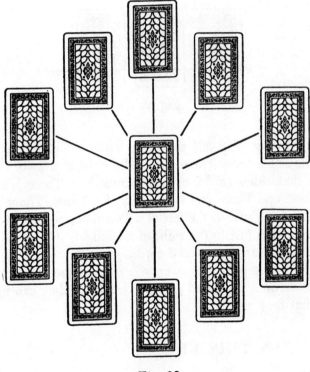

Fig. 28

See if you can put one card in the center and the other 10 cards around it in a circle (Fig. 28), so that the spots of every line or row of 3 cards stretching from one side of the circle through the center to the other side will add up to 18.

A CARD BRAIN-TWISTER

This is a puzzle that you can figure out, but you have to be really pretty good to guess it. Take the statements one by one, figure out each one's possibilities, and see how well you can do.

Fig. 29

The drawing (Fig. 29) shows the backs of 3 playing cards. There is at least one Three just to the right of a Two. (That means that either card 2 or card 3 must be a Three.) There is at least one Three just to the left of a Three. There is at least one Club just to the left of a Diamond, and there is at least one Club just to the right of a Club.

See if you can name the 3 cards.

When you know the answer, you can put the actual cards face down on a table and ask your friends if they can figure out what they are.

HOW CAN THIS BE?

Hold a pack of cards in your hand, and tell a friend the following story. A boy once dealt some cards to his three brothers. To the oldest he gave half the cards and half a card. He then gave half of the cards he had left and half a card to the second brother. Finally he gave half of the cards he then had left and half a card to his youngest brother. He then had no cards left.

At no time was a card cut, torn, or divided in any way. How many cards did he have at first? You proceed to show your friend by dealing out cards just as the boy did in the puzzle.

CARD PICKUP PUZZLE

Put 9 cards on the table arranged in 3 rows of 3 cards each, to form a square (Fig. 30). Then ask someone if he can pick up all the cards in 4 *continuous* straight lines. That is: He

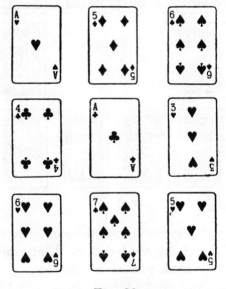

Fig. 30

must start at one card and pick up the line of cards of which it is the first one; the next line must start with a card next to the last card picked up, and the last two lines must start the same way. The lines may be straight across, up and down, or diagonal.

TURN OVER ALL BUT ONE

Put 10 cards face down on a table, arranged as shown in the drawing (Fig. 31). The puzzle then is to start at any face-down card counting it as 1, skip over 2 cards, counting clockwise, and turn the fourth card face up. You leave the card counted as 1 face down.

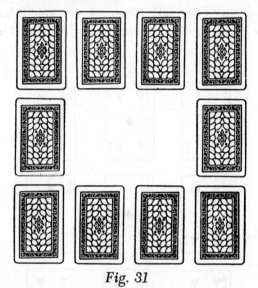

Fig. 31

You then pick another face-down card—any one—and do the same thing, turning the fourth card face up. Then continue until all the cards but one are face up.

You must always count a face-down card as 1 and land on a face-down card as the fourth card. If you don't know the secret, you will run out of face-down cards to use as the first and the fourth, before you reach the solution.

THE GIVE-AND-TAKE PUZZLE

A boy and a girl, Bill and Betty, each had a certain number of cards. Bill gave Betty as many cards as she already had.

When Betty received these cards, she asked Bill how many cards he had left, and promptly gave this number of cards back to Bill. Bill, not wishing to be greedy, gave Betty back as many cards as Betty had left. This left Bill without any cards and gave Betty 8 cards altogether. How many cards did each one have in the beginning?

ODD OR EVEN?

Give a friend a pack of cards and ask him to remove 2 piles—one containing an odd number of cards such as 3, 5 or 7, and the other containing an even number of cards such as 2, 4 or 6.

Ask him to hold 1 pile in his right hand and the other in his left hand, but not to let you know which hand holds which pile.

Now tell him to multiply the number of cards in his right hand by 3 and the number in his left hand by 2. Ask him to add these two products and to tell you whether the sum is an odd or even number. You can then tell him in which hand he is holding the odd number of cards and in which hand the even number.

THE TWENTY-FOUR CARD PUZZLE

This puzzle—or game—for it is both a puzzle and a game, is good for hours of fun. You can do it over and over again, each time in a different way, trying to get the best possible score for yourself, and you can also play against a friend who works the puzzle with a second pack of cards.

Put 24 cards on the table, arranged as in the drawing (Fig. 32). To start, pick up one of the cards two spaces from the center, like the one marked A, put it in the empty center space, and take out the card it "jumped" (B in the drawing).

Then jump any other card over another into an empty space
and remove the card you jump each time.

The object is to remove as many cards as possible by jumping up, down, or across, but never jumping diagonally. If two
people are playing, the winner is the one who has the fewest
cards left when he can make no more jumps. If you can finish
with only one card left, you are a marvel.

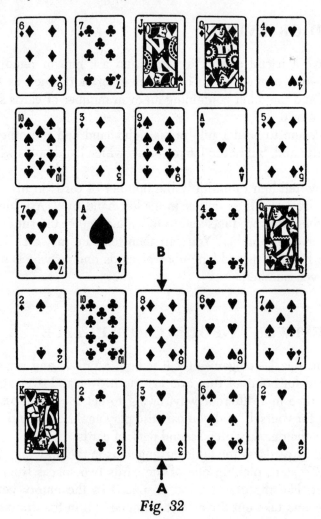

Fig. 32

SILLY SAM'S PACK OF CARDS

Silly Sam thought he would play cards one rainy afternoon, and decided to fix up an entirely new kind of pack. He made a pack of 33 cards, of which some were, naturally, red, and the others black.

In his pack there were 3 black to every 2 red cards among the plain cards; and 5 black to every 3 red cards among the face cards.

How many of each kind of card were there in the pack?

THE REVERSE-ORDER PUZZLE

This is one of the best of all card puzzles and, like "The Twenty-Four Card Puzzle," can be played a good deal like a game.

THE START

Fig. 33

Eleven cards, running from an Ace to a Jack, are arranged in 3 rows as shown in the drawing (Fig. 33). The puzzle then is to move the cards so as to reverse their order, ending up with the cards arranged as in the second drawing (Fig. 34).

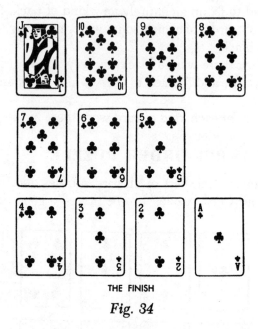

THE FINISH

Fig. 34

The first move is to move either the Eight or the Jack into the empty space in the lower right-hand corner. Then move one card at a time into any space next to it. The cards may be moved straight across and up and down, but never diagonally.

The solution is given in the "Answers" section.

CARD LEAPFROG PUZZLE

Put 12 cards on the table, arranged as shown in the drawing (Fig. 35) in 3 rows of 4 cards each. Put an Ace at the left-hand end of the top row.

The puzzle now is to remove all the cards from the table

except the Ace, by jumping one card over the other as in checkers and removing the cards jumped over. At the end, the Ace is to be back in its original position.

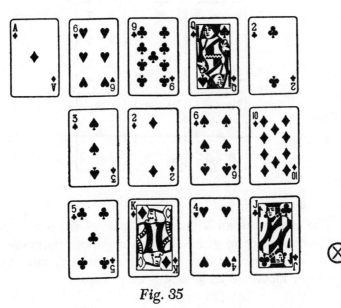

Fig. 35

The circle with an X inside it is part of the puzzle and permits the first jump to be made. It is the only spot outside the puzzle, however, to which a card may be moved.

PUT-THEM-IN-ORDER PUZZLE

This is one of the classic "switching" puzzles, in which you have to move the cards about to rearrange them in a different order.

You start by putting on the table 6 cards, running from an Ace to a Six, arranged as shown in the drawing (Fig. 36). The puzzle is to shift the cards one at a time, until they are arranged in proper numerical order, with the Ace, Two and

Three in the top row, and the Four, Five and Six in the bottom row.

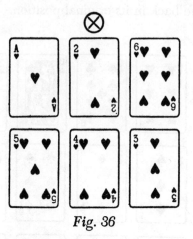

Fig. 36

The circle with an X inside it is part of the puzzle, for it is the only place to which the first move can be made. The cards are not jumped over one another. At each move a card is simply moved to an adjoining empty space.

ACE-TWO-THREE-FOUR PUZZLE

Take an Ace and a Two, Three and Four from the pack and put them face up in a pile on the table. Put the Four on the bottom of the pile, then the Three, then the Two, and the Ace on top.

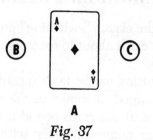

Fig. 37

Consider that the cards are on spot A, and that spots B and C are to the left and right, respectively, as in the drawing (Fig. 37). The puzzle is to move the cards one at a time so that finally they are all on spot C in the same order as they were on spot A. They can be moved to right or left, and over the cards in the middle, if necessary, but according to these rules:

1. A card may be moved only to an empty spot or
2. To a spot with a higher value card in the pile.
   The higher value card does not have to be the top card.
3. Make no more than 13 moves.

Solutions to Puzzles
with Cards

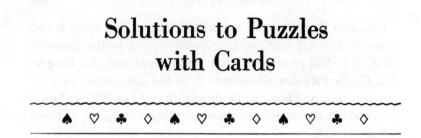

CHANGING THE ROWS

The solution is as follows:

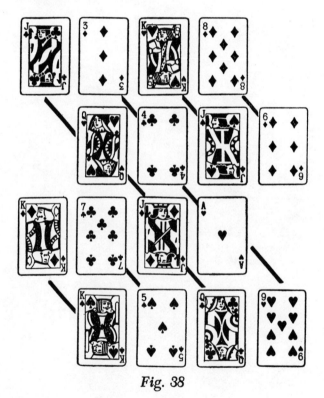

Fig. 38

Move the first left-hand card of the second row from the top over to the right, and do the same with the first left-hand card of the bottom row. Then count the two face cards at the lower left-hand corner as the first row, and so on. The catch is that the rows in the solution are on a slant.

THE ADD-TO-18 PUZZLE

Here is how you arrange the cards:

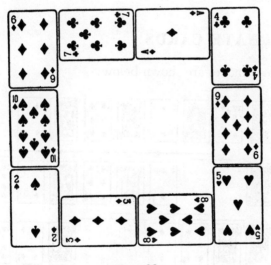

Fig. 39

THREE-IN-A-ROW

Move the card at the left over to the right end of the row. This changes the position of the original middle card and puts it—without touching it—at the left end of the row.

THE SIXTEEN-CARD PUZZLE

The cards are arranged as follows:
Jack of Diamonds—Queen of Clubs—King of Hearts—Ace of Spades.

King of Spades—Ace of Hearts—Jack of Clubs—Queen of Diamonds.

Ace of Clubs—King of Diamonds—Queen of Spades—Jack of Hearts.

Queen of Hearts—Jack of Spades—Ace of Diamonds—King of Clubs.

ALTERNATE CARDS

The four moves are shown below:

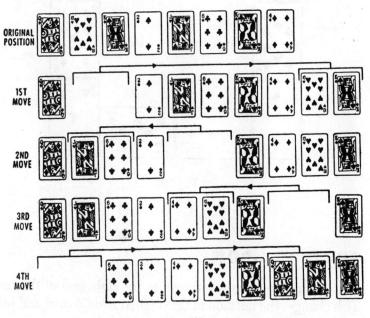

Fig. 40

THE FIVE-KINGS PUZZLE

Counting from the left, give each card a number, from 1 to 10 (Fig. 41). Put card number 4 on card number 1; then put 6 on 9; 8 on 3; 2 on 5; and 7 on 10.

Fig. 41

THE NOBLE LORDS AND THE COMMONERS

You need to touch with your hand only the center card in the top row. Pick it up and put it down again just beneath the center card in the bottom row. Then push up the entire middle column until the card you are touching becomes the center card of the bottom row.

TRICKY TRIANGLE

Give the cards numbers from top to bottom as shown in the drawing (Fig. 42). Move card 7 to the left of card 2; card 10 to the right of card 3; and card 1 to a point below and between cards 8 and 9.

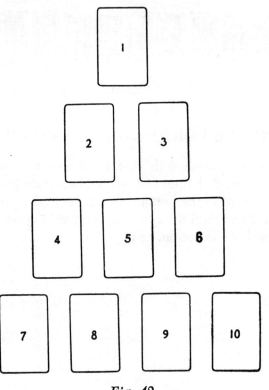

Fig. 42

FACE-UP

The cards are identified in the drawing below (Fig. 43) by the numbers 1, 2 and 3. The 3 moves are as follows. On the first move, turn over cards 2 and 3, turning card 2 face down and card 3 face up. On the second move, turn over

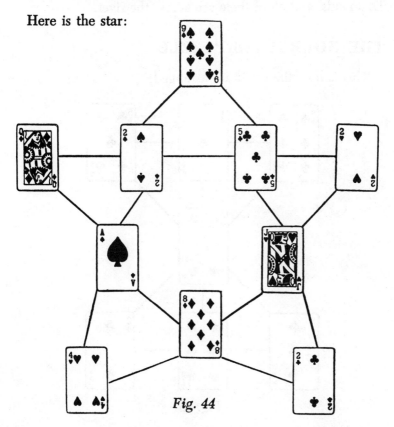

Fig. 43

cards 1 and 3. On the third and last move, turn over cards 2 and 3. All 3 cards will then be face up.

THE STAR PUZZLE

Here is the star:

Fig. 44

THE JEALOUS KINGS

The King and Queen of Clubs go over first. The King of Clubs then returns alone.

The Queen of Hearts and the Queen of Diamonds go over. The Queen of Clubs returns by herself, and the King of Hearts and the King of Diamonds go over.

The King and Queen of Hearts return. The King of Clubs and the King of Hearts go over. The Queen of Diamonds returns alone.

The Queen of Clubs and the Queen of Hearts go over. The King of Diamonds then returns and takes over the Queen of Diamonds, and all of them are across the river.

THE HOURGLASS PUZZLE

This is how the cards are arranged:

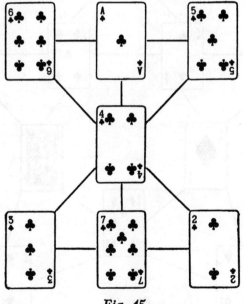

Fig. 45

THE EIGHTEEN-CARD CIRCLE

This is how you arrange the cards:

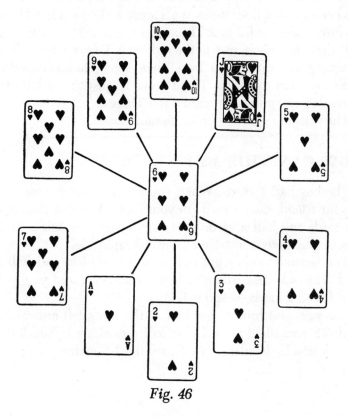

Fig. 46

A CARD BRAIN-TWISTER

The cards are:
1. The Two of Clubs
2. The Three of Clubs
3. The Three of Diamonds

The reasoning goes this way. There is at least one Three just to the right of a Two. That means that either card 2 or card 3 is a Three, because they are the only cards to the right of another card.

There is at least one Three just to the left of a Three. That means that either card 1 or card 2 is a Three. Since card 2 has been spotted both times as a Three, we know it is a Three.

Now, since card 2 is a Three and the first statement says that there is a Three just to the right of a Two, we are safe in assuming that card 1 is a Two. Then, since the second statement says that there is a Three (card 2) just to the left of a Three, we can guess that card 3 is a Three.

The suits are figured out in the same manner.

HOW CAN THIS BE?

The boy had 7 cards. When you are showing the solution to your friend, take 7 cards in your hand. You first deal half the cards and half a card. That is 3½ cards plus half a card, or 4. So you give your friend 4 cards, keeping 3.

The second brother got half of the cards left and half a card. This was 1½ cards plus half a card, or 2 and you give your friend 2 cards, keeping 1.

The youngest brother got half of the cards left and half a card. This was half a card plus half a card, or 1. You finish the solution by handing your friend the 1 remaining card.

CARD PICKUP PUZZLE

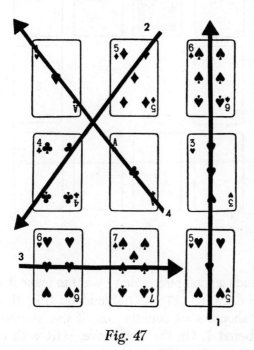

Fig. 47

The drawing shows the 4 continuous straight lines.

TURN OVER ALL BUT ONE

The solution of this puzzle is simple, and is easy to remember. It is this: Always arrange your starting point—each card number 1—so that you will turn face up the card that was the starting point of the preceding move.

The first card number 1 may be any card. It doesn't matter. But on your second move, make card number 1 the card 3 cards in a counter-clockwise direction away from the first card number 1. Then you will turn face up the first card number 1, which is in accordance with the formula given above.

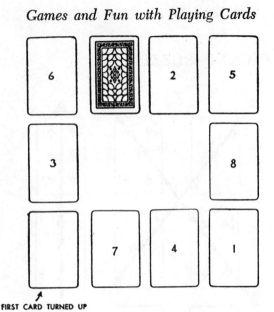

FIRST CARD TURNED UP

Fig. 48

This is such a good puzzle that I want to make it absolutely clear. The drawing (Fig. 48) should do this. It shows the cards you should start counting on, if you started with the card numbered 1. On the next move, start with card 2, on the next move with card 3, and so on.

THE GIVE-AND-TAKE PUZZLE

Bill had 5 cards, and Betty had 3. It is fun to take 5 cards yourself and give 3 to a friend and go through the different givings and takings to watch the puzzle work out.

ODD OR EVEN?

If the number he tells you is an even number, he is holding the even number of cards in his right hand. If it is an odd number, he is holding the odd number of cards in his right hand.

SILLY SAM'S PACK OF CARDS

There were 15 black and 10 red cards in the plain card part of the pack, and 5 black and 3 red cards in the face card part.

THE REVERSE-ORDER PUZZLE

The winning moves are as follows. Each card named is moved into a space that you will find empty next to it:

Jack, 10, 9, 5, 6, 7, 8.

Jack, 10, 9, 5, 6, Ace, 2, 3, 4.

Jack, 10, 9, 5, 6, Ace, 2, 3, 4.

Jack, 10, 9, 5, 6, Ace, 2, 3, 4.

Jack, 10, 9, 8, 6, Ace, 2, 3, 4.

Jack, 10, 9, 8, 5, Ace, 2, 3, 4.

7, 6, 5.

CARD LEAPFROG PUZZLE

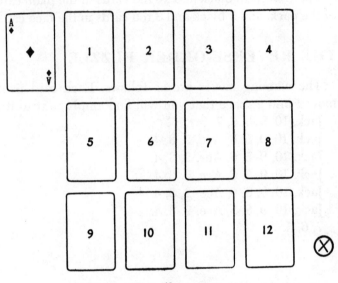

Fig. 49

The cards are numbered in this drawing (Fig. 49) so that you can follow the moves. These are as follows:

1. Jump 11 over 12 to X. Remove 12.
2. Jump 9 over 10 to 11. Remove 10.
3. Jump 2 over 6 to 10. Remove 6.
4. Jump 4 over 8 to 12. Remove 8.
5. Jump the Ace over 1 to 2, then over 3 to 4. Remove 1 and 3.
6. Jump 11 over 7 to 3. Remove 7.
7. Jump X over 12 to 11, then over 10 to 9, then over 5 to 1. Remove 12, 10 and 5.
8. Jump 4 (the Ace) over 3 to 2, and then over 1 to its original position. Remove 3 and 1.

PUT-THEM-IN-ORDER PUZZLE

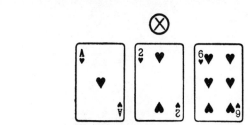

Fig. 50

On each move there will be only one space open to which a card can be shifted. Move the cards in the following order: Two to X, Four, Three, Six, Four, Three, Five, Ace, Three, Four, Six, Five, Four, Three, Ace, Four, Five, Six, Three, Two.

ACE-TWO-THREE-FOUR PUZZLE

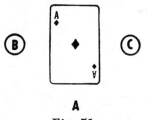

A

Fig. 51

The moves are made as follows; reading down:

Ace to B	Ace to B	Two to A	Ace to B
Two to C	Two to B	Ace to A	Two to C
Ace to C	Four to C	Three to C	Ace to C
Three to B			

PUT THEM IN ORDER PUZZLE

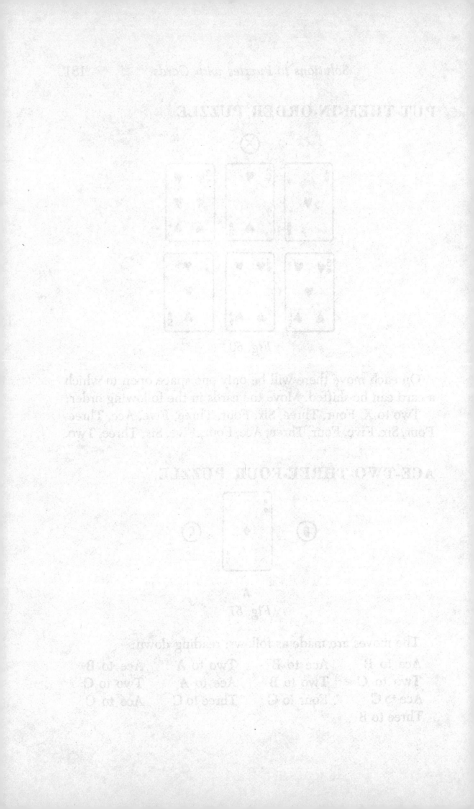

Fig. 86

On each move there will be only one space open in which a card can be dalled. Move to cards in the following order: Two to X, Four, Three, Six, Four, Three, Five, Ace, Three, Four, Six, Five, Four, Three, Ace, Four, Five, Ace, Three, Two.

ACE-TWO-THREE-FOUR PUZZLE

Fig. 87

The moves are made as follows, reading down:

Ace to B	Ace to B	Two to A	Ace to B
Two to C	Two to D	Ace to D	Two to C
Ace to C	Four to C	Three to C	Ace to C
Three to B			

Index

A CATALOGUE OF
SELECTED DOVER BOOKS
IN ALL FIELDS OF INTEREST

A CATALOGUE OF SELECTED DOVER
BOOKS IN ALL FIELDS OF INTEREST

RACKHAM'S COLOR ILLUSTRATIONS FOR WAGNER'S RING. Rackham's finest mature work—all 64 full-color watercolors in a faithful and lush interpretation of the *Ring*. Full-sized plates on coated stock of the paintings used by opera companies for authentic staging of Wagner. Captions aid in following complete Ring cycle. Introduction. 64 illustrations plus vignettes. 72pp. 8⅝ x 11¼. 23779-6 Pa. $6.00

CONTEMPORARY POLISH POSTERS IN FULL COLOR, edited by Joseph Czestochowski. 46 full-color examples of brilliant school of Polish graphic design, selected from world's first museum (near Warsaw) dedicated to poster art. Posters on circuses, films, plays, concerts all show cosmopolitan influences, free imagination. Introduction. 48pp. 9⅜ x 12¼. 23780-X Pa. $6.00

GRAPHIC WORKS OF EDVARD MUNCH, Edvard Munch. 90 haunting, evocative prints by first major Expressionist artist and one of the greatest graphic artists of his time: *The Scream, Anxiety, Death Chamber, The Kiss, Madonna,* etc. Introduction by Alfred Werner. 90pp. 9 x 12. 23765-6 Pa. $5.00

THE GOLDEN AGE OF THE POSTER, Hayward and Blanche Cirker. 70 extraordinary posters in full colors, from Maitres de l'Affiche, Mucha, Lautrec, Bradley, Cheret, Beardsley, many others. Total of 78pp. 9⅜ x 12¼. 22753-7 Pa. $5.95

THE NOTEBOOKS OF LEONARDO DA VINCI, edited by J. P. Richter. Extracts from manuscripts reveal great genius; on painting, sculpture, anatomy, sciences, geography, etc. Both Italian and English. 186 ms. pages reproduced, plus 500 additional drawings, including studies for *Last Supper,* Sforza monument, etc. 860pp. 7⅞ x 10¾. (Available in U.S. only) 22572-0, 22573-9 Pa., Two-vol. set $15.90

THE CODEX NUTTALL, as first edited by Zelia Nuttall. Only inexpensive edition, in full color, of a pre-Columbian Mexican (Mixtec) book. 88 color plates show kings, gods, heroes, temples, sacrifices. New explanatory, historical introduction by Arthur G. Miller. 96pp. 11⅜ x 8½. (Available in U.S. only) 23168-2 Pa. $7.95

UNE SEMAINE DE BONTÉ, A SURREALISTIC NOVEL IN COLLAGE, Max Ernst. Masterpiece created out of 19th-century periodical illustrations, explores worlds of terror and surprise. Some consider this Ernst's greatest work. 208pp. 8⅛ x 11. 23252-2 Pa. $5.00

DRAWINGS OF WILLIAM BLAKE, William Blake. 92 plates from Book of Job, *Divine Comedy, Paradise Lost,* visionary heads, mythological figures, Laocoon, etc. Selection, introduction, commentary by Sir Geoffrey Keynes. 178pp. 8⅛ x 11. 22303-5 Pa. $4.00

ENGRAVINGS OF HOGARTH, William Hogarth. 101 of Hogarth's greatest works: *Rake's Progress, Harlot's Progress, Illustrations for Hudibras, Before and After, Beer Street and Gin Lane,* many more. Full commentary. 256pp. 11 x 13¾. 22479-1 Pa. $12.95

DAUMIER: 120 GREAT LITHOGRAPHS, Honore Daumier. Wide-ranging collection of lithographs by the greatest caricaturist of the 19th century. Concentrates on eternally popular series on lawyers, on married life, on liberated women, etc. Selection, introduction, and notes on plates by Charles F. Ramus. Total of 158pp. 9⅜ x 12¼. 23512-2 Pa. $5.50

DRAWINGS OF MUCHA, Alphonse Maria Mucha. Work reveals draftsman of highest caliber: studies for famous posters and paintings, renderings for book illustrations and ads, etc. 70 works, 9 in color; including 6 items not drawings. Introduction. List of illustrations. 72pp. 9⅜ x 12¼. (Available in U.S. only) 23672-2 Pa. $4.00

GIOVANNI BATTISTA PIRANESI: DRAWINGS IN THE PIERPONT MORGAN LIBRARY, Giovanni Battista Piranesi. For first time ever all of Morgan Library's collection, world's largest. 167 illustrations of rare Piranesi drawings—archeological, architectural, decorative and visionary. Essay, detailed list of drawings, chronology, captions. Edited by Felice Stampfle. 144pp. 9⅜ x 12¼. 23714-1 Pa. $7.50

NEW YORK ETCHINGS (1905-1949), John Sloan. All of important American artist's N.Y. life etchings. 67 works include some of his best art; also lively historical record—Greenwich Village, tenement scenes. Edited by Sloan's widow. Introduction and captions. 79pp. 8⅜ x 11¼. 23651-X Pa. $4.00

CHINESE PAINTING AND CALLIGRAPHY: A PICTORIAL SURVEY, Wan-go Weng. 69 fine examples from John M. Crawford's matchless private collection: landscapes, birds, flowers, human figures, etc., plus calligraphy. Every basic form included: hanging scrolls, handscrolls, album leaves, fans, etc. 109 illustrations. Introduction. Captions. 192pp. 8⅞ x 11¾. 23707-9 Pa. $7.95

DRAWINGS OF REMBRANDT, edited by Seymour Slive. Updated Lippmann, Hofstede de Groot edition, with definitive scholarly apparatus. All portraits, biblical sketches, landscapes, nudes, Oriental figures, classical studies, together with selection of work by followers. 550 illustrations. Total of 630pp. 9⅛ x 12¼. 21485-0, 21486-9 Pa., Two-vol. set $15.00

THE DISASTERS OF WAR, Francisco Goya. 83 etchings record horrors of Napoleonic wars in Spain and war in general. Reprint of 1st edition, plus 3 additional plates. Introduction by Philip Hofer. 97pp. 9⅜ x 8¼. 21872-4 Pa. $3.75

THE EARLY WORK OF AUBREY BEARDSLEY, Aubrey Beardsley. 157 plates, 2 in color: *Manon Lescaut, Madame Bovary, Morte Darthur, Salome,* other. Introduction by H. Marillier. 182pp. 8⅛ x 11. 21816-3 Pa. $4.50

THE LATER WORK OF AUBREY BEARDSLEY, Aubrey Beardsley. Exotic masterpieces of full maturity: *Venus and Tannhauser, Lysistrata, Rape of the Lock, Volpone,* Savoy material, etc. 174 plates, 2 in color. 186pp. 8⅛ x 11. 21817-1 Pa. $4.50

THOMAS NAST'S CHRISTMAS DRAWINGS, Thomas Nast. Almost all Christmas drawings by creator of image of Santa Claus as we know it, and one of America's foremost illustrators and political cartoonists. 66 illustrations. 3 illustrations in color on covers. 96pp. 8⅜ x 11¼. 23660-9 Pa. $3.50

THE DORÉ ILLUSTRATIONS FOR DANTE'S DIVINE COMEDY, Gustave Doré. All 135 plates from Inferno, Purgatory, Paradise; fantastic tortures, infernal landscapes, celestial wonders. Each plate with appropriate (translated) verses. 141pp. 9 x 12. 23231-X Pa. $4.50

DORÉ'S ILLUSTRATIONS FOR RABELAIS, Gustave Doré. 252 striking illustrations of *Gargantua and Pantagruel* books by foremost 19th-century illustrator. Including 60 plates, 192 delightful smaller illustrations. 153pp. 9 x 12. 23656-0 Pa. $5.00

LONDON: A PILGRIMAGE, Gustave Doré, Blanchard Jerrold. Squalor, riches, misery, beauty of mid-Victorian metropolis; 55 wonderful plates, 125 other illustrations, full social, cultural text by Jerrold. 191pp. of text. 9⅜ x 12¼. 22306-X Pa. $7.00

THE RIME OF THE ANCIENT MARINER, Gustave Doré, S. T. Coleridge. Dore's finest work, 34 plates capture moods, subtleties of poem. Full text. Introduction by Millicent Rose. 77pp. 9¼ x 12. 22305-1 Pa. $3.50

THE DORE BIBLE ILLUSTRATIONS, Gustave Doré. All wonderful, detailed plates: Adam and Eve, Flood, Babylon, Life of Jesus, etc. Brief King James text with each plate. Introduction by Millicent Rose. 241 plates. 241pp. 9 x 12. 23004-X Pa. $6.00

THE COMPLETE ENGRAVINGS, ETCHINGS AND DRYPOINTS OF ALBRECHT DURER. "Knight, Death and Devil"; "Melencolia," and more—all Dürer's known works in all three media, including 6 works formerly attributed to him. 120 plates. 235pp. 8⅜ x 11¼. 22851-7 Pa. $6.50

MAXIMILIAN'S TRIUMPHAL ARCH, Albrecht Dürer and others. Incredible monument of woodcut art: 8 foot high elaborate arch—heraldic figures, humans, battle scenes, fantastic elements—that you can assemble yourself. Printed on one side, layout for assembly. 143pp. 11 x 16. 21451-6 Pa. $5.00

CATALOGUE OF DOVER BOOKS

THE COMPLETE WOODCUTS OF ALBRECHT DURER, edited by Dr. W. Kurth. 346 in all: "Old Testament," "St. Jerome," "Passion," "Life of Virgin," Apocalypse," many others. Introduction by Campbell Dodgson. 285pp. 8½ x 12¼. 21097-9 Pa. $7.50

DRAWINGS OF ALBRECHT DURER, edited by Heinrich Wolfflin. 81 plates show development from youth to full style. Many favorites; many new. Introduction by Alfred Werner. 96pp. 8⅛ x 11. 22352-3 Pa. $5.00

THE HUMAN FIGURE, Albrecht Dürer. Experiments in various techniques—stereometric, progressive proportional, and others. Also life studies that rank among finest ever done. Complete reprinting of Dresden Sketchbook. 170 plates. 355pp. 8⅜ x 11¼. 21042-1 Pa. $7.95

OF THE JUST SHAPING OF LETTERS, Albrecht Dürer. Renaissance artist explains design of Roman majuscules by geometry, also Gothic lower and capitals. Grolier Club edition. 43pp. 7⅞ x 10¾ 21306-4 Pa. $3.00

TEN BOOKS ON ARCHITECTURE, Vitruvius. The most important book ever written on architecture. Early Roman aesthetics, technology, classical orders, site selection, all other aspects. Stands behind everything since. Morgan translation. 331pp. 5⅜ x 8½. 20645-9 Pa. $4.50

THE FOUR BOOKS OF ARCHITECTURE, Andrea Palladio. 16th-century classic responsible for Palladian movement and style. Covers classical architectural remains, Renaissance revivals, classical orders, etc. 1738 Ware English edition. Introduction by A. Placzek. 216 plates. 110pp. of text. 9½ x 12¾. 21308-0 Pa. $10.00

HORIZONS, Norman Bel Geddes. Great industrialist stage designer, "father of streamlining," on application of aesthetics to transportation, amusement, architecture, etc. 1932 prophetic account; function, theory, specific projects. 222 illustrations. 312pp. 7⅞ x 10¾. 23514-9 Pa. $6.95

FRANK LLOYD WRIGHT'S FALLINGWATER, Donald Hoffmann. Full, illustrated story of conception and building of Wright's masterwork at Bear Run, Pa. 100 photographs of site, construction, and details of completed structure. 112pp. 9¼ x 10. 23671-4 Pa. $5.50

THE ELEMENTS OF DRAWING, John Ruskin. Timeless classic by great Viltorian; starts with basic ideas, works through more difficult. Many practical exercises. 48 illustrations. Introduction by Lawrence Campbell. 228pp. 5⅜ x 8½. 22730-8 Pa. $3.75

GIST OF ART, John Sloan. Greatest modern American teacher, Art Students League, offers innumerable hints, instructions, guided comments to help you in painting. Not a formal course. 46 illustrations. Introduction by Helen Sloan. 200pp. 5⅜ x 8½. 23435-5 Pa. $4.00

THE ANATOMY OF THE HORSE, George Stubbs. Often considered the great masterpiece of animal anatomy. Full reproduction of 1766 edition, plus prospectus; original text and modernized text. 36 plates. Introduction by Eleanor Garvey. 121pp. 11 x 14¾.   23402-9 Pa. $6.00

BRIDGMAN'S LIFE DRAWING, George B. Bridgman. More than 500 illustrative drawings and text teach you to abstract the body into its major masses, use light and shade, proportion; as well as specific areas of anatomy, of which Bridgman is master. 192pp. 6½ x 9¼. (Available in U.S. only)
22710-3 Pa. $3.50

ART NOUVEAU DESIGNS IN COLOR, Alphonse Mucha, Maurice Verneuil, Georges Auriol. Full-color reproduction of *Combinaisons ornementales* (c. 1900) by Art Nouveau masters. Floral, animal, geometric, interlacings, swashes—borders, frames, spots—all incredibly beautiful. 60 plates, hundreds of designs. 9⅜ x 8-1/16.   22885-1 Pa. $4.00

FULL-COLOR FLORAL DESIGNS IN THE ART NOUVEAU STYLE, E. A. Seguy. 166 motifs, on 40 plates, from *Les fleurs et leurs applications decoratives* (1902): borders, circular designs, repeats, allovers, "spots." All in authentic Art Nouveau colors. 48pp. 9⅜ x 12¼.
23439-8 Pa. $5.00

A DIDEROT PICTORIAL ENCYCLOPEDIA OF TRADES AND INDUSTRY, edited by Charles C. Gillispie. 485 most interesting plates from the great French Encyclopedia of the 18th century show hundreds of working figures, artifacts, process, land and cityscapes; glassmaking, papermaking, metal extraction, construction, weaving, making furniture, clothing, wigs, dozens of other activities. Plates fully explained. 920pp. 9 x 12.
22284-5, 22285-3 Clothbd., Two-vol. set $40.00

HANDBOOK OF EARLY ADVERTISING ART, Clarence P. Hornung. Largest collection of copyright-free early and antique advertising art ever compiled. Over 6,000 illustrations, from Franklin's time to the 1890's for special effects, novelty. Valuable source, almost inexhaustible.
Pictorial Volume. Agriculture, the zodiac, animals, autos, birds, Christmas, fire engines, flowers, trees, musical instruments, ships, games and sports, much more. Arranged by subject matter and use. 237 plates. 288pp. 9 x 12.
20122-8 Clothbd. $14.50

Typographical Volume. Roman and Gothic faces ranging from 10 point to 300 point, "Barnum," German and Old English faces, script, logotypes, scrolls and flourishes, 1115 ornamental initials, 67 complete alphabets, more. 310 plates. 320pp. 9 x 12.   20123-6 Clothbd. $15.00

CALLIGRAPHY (CALLIGRAPHIA LATINA), J. G. Schwandner. High point of 18th-century ornamental calligraphy. Very ornate initials, scrolls, borders, cherubs, birds, lettered examples. 172pp. 9 x 13.
20475-8 Pa. $7.00

CATALOGUE OF DOVER BOOKS

ART FORMS IN NATURE, Ernst Haeckel. Multitude of strangely beautiful natural forms: Radiolaria, Foraminifera, jellyfishes, fungi, turtles, bats, etc. All 100 plates of the 19th-century evolutionist's *Kunstformen der Natur* (1904). 100pp. 9⅜ x 12¼. 22987-4 Pa. $5.00

CHILDREN: A PICTORIAL ARCHIVE FROM NINETEENTH-CENTURY SOURCES, edited by Carol Belanger Grafton. 242 rare, copyright-free wood engravings for artists and designers. Widest such selection available. All illustrations in line. 119pp. 8⅜ x 11¼. 23694-3 Pa. $3.50

WOMEN: A PICTORIAL ARCHIVE FROM NINETEENTH-CENTURY SOURCES, edited by Jim Harter. 391 copyright-free wood engravings for artists and designers selected from rare periodicals. Most extensive such collection available. All illustrations in line. 128pp. 9 x 12. 23703-6 Pa. $4.50

ARABIC ART IN COLOR, Prisse d'Avennes. From the greatest ornamentalists of all time—50 plates in color, rarely seen outside the Near East, rich in suggestion and stimulus. Includes 4 plates on covers. 46pp. 9⅜ x 12¼. 23658-7 Pa. $6.00

AUTHENTIC ALGERIAN CARPET DESIGNS AND MOTIFS, edited by June Beveridge. Algerian carpets are world famous. Dozens of geometrical motifs are charted on grids, color-coded, for weavers, needleworkers, craftsmen, designers. 53 illustrations plus 4 in color. 48pp. 8¼ x 11. (Available in U.S. only) 23650-1 Pa. $1.75

DICTIONARY OF AMERICAN PORTRAITS, edited by Hayward and Blanche Cirker. 4000 important Americans, earliest times to 1905, mostly in clear line. Politicians, writers, soldiers, scientists, inventors, industrialists, Indians, Blacks, women, outlaws, etc. Identificatory information. 756pp. 9¼ x 12¾. 21823-6 Clothbd. $40.00

HOW THE OTHER HALF LIVES, Jacob A. Riis. Journalistic record of filth, degradation, upward drive in New York immigrant slums, shops, around 1900. New edition includes 100 original Riis photos, monuments of early photography. 233pp. 10 x 7⅞. 22012-5 Pa. $7.00

NEW YORK IN THE THIRTIES, Berenice Abbott. Noted photographer's fascinating study of city shows new buildings that have become famous and old sights that have disappeared forever. Insightful commentary. 97 photographs. 97pp. 11⅜ x 10. 22967-X Pa. $5.00

MEN AT WORK, Lewis W. Hine. Famous photographic studies of construction workers, railroad men, factory workers and coal miners. New supplement of 18 photos on Empire State building construction. New introduction by Jonathan L. Doherty. Total of 69 photos. 63pp. 8 x 10¾. 23475-4 Pa. $3.00

THE DEPRESSION YEARS AS PHOTOGRAPHED BY ARTHUR ROTH-STEIN, Arthur Rothstein. First collection devoted entirely to the work of outstanding 1930s photographer: famous dust storm photo, ragged children, unemployed, etc. 120 photographs. Captions. 119pp. 9¼ x 10¾.

23590-4 Pa. $5.00

CAMERA WORK: A PICTORIAL GUIDE, Alfred Stieglitz. All 559 illustrations and plates from the most important periodical in the history of art photography, Camera Work (1903-17). Presented four to a page, reduced in size but still clear, in strict chronological order, with complete captions. Three indexes. Glossary. Bibliography. 176pp. 8⅜ x 11¼.

23591-2 Pa. $6.95

ALVIN LANGDON COBURN, PHOTOGRAPHER, Alvin L. Coburn. Revealing autobiography by one of greatest photographers of 20th century gives insider's version of Photo-Secession, plus comments on his own work. 77 photographs by Coburn. Edited by Helmut and Alison Gernsheim. 160pp. 8⅛ x 11.

23685-4 Pa. $6.00

NEW YORK IN THE FORTIES, Andreas Feininger. 162 brilliant photographs by the well-known photographer, formerly with Life magazine, show commuters, shoppers, Times Square at night, Harlem nightclub, Lower East Side, etc. Introduction and full captions by John von Hartz. 181pp. 9¼ x 10¾.

23585-8 Pa. $6.00

GREAT NEWS PHOTOS AND THE STORIES BEHIND THEM, John Faber. Dramatic volume of 140 great news photos, 1855 through 1976, and revealing stories behind them, with both historical and technical information. Hindenburg disaster, shooting of Oswald, nomination of Jimmy Carter, etc. 160pp. 8¼ x 11.

23667-6 Pa. $5.00

THE ART OF THE CINEMATOGRAPHER, Leonard Maltin. Survey of American cinematography history and anecdotal interviews with 5 masters—Arthur Miller, Hal Mohr, Hal Rosson, Lucien Ballard, and Conrad Hall. Very large selection of behind-the-scenes production photos. 105 photographs. Filmographies. Index. Originally Behind the Camera. 144pp. 8¼ x 11.

23686-2 Pa. $5.00

DESIGNS FOR THE THREE-CORNERED HAT (LE TRICORNE), Pablo Picasso. 32 fabulously rare drawings—including 31 color illustrations of costumes and accessories—for 1919 production of famous ballet. Edited by Parmenia Migel, who has written new introduction. 48pp. 9⅜ x 12¼. (Available in U.S. only)

23709-5 Pa. $5.00

NOTES OF A FILM DIRECTOR, Sergei Eisenstein. Greatest Russian filmmaker explains montage, making of Alexander Nevsky, aesthetics; comments on self, associates, great rivals (Chaplin), similar material. 78 illustrations. 240pp. 5⅜ x 8½.

22392-2 Pa. $4.50

HOLLYWOOD GLAMOUR PORTRAITS, edited by John Kobal. 145 photos capture the stars from 1926-49, the high point in portrait photography. Gable, Harlow, Bogart, Bacall, Hedy Lamarr, Marlene Dietrich, Robert Montgomery, Marlon Brando, Veronica Lake; 94 stars in all. Full background on photographers, technical aspects, much more. Total of 160pp. 8⅜ x 11¼.   23352-9 Pa. **$6.00**

THE NEW YORK STAGE: FAMOUS PRODUCTIONS IN PHOTO-GRAPHS, edited by Stanley Appelbaum. 148 photographs from Museum of City of New York show 142 plays, 1883-1939. *Peter Pan, The Front Page, Dead End, Our Town,* O'Neill, hundreds of actors and actresses, etc. Full indexes. 154pp. 9½ x 10.   23241-7 Pa. $6.00

DIALOGUES CONCERNING TWO NEW SCIENCES, Galileo Galilei. Encompassing 30 years of experiment and thought, these dialogues deal with geometric demonstrations of fracture of solid bodies, cohesion, leverage, speed of light and sound, pendulums, falling bodies, accelerated motion, etc. 300pp. 5⅜ x 8½.   60099-8 Pa. $4.00

THE GREAT OPERA STARS IN HISTORIC PHOTOGRAPHS, edited by James Camner. 343 portraits from the 1850s to the 1940s: Tamburini, Mario, Caliapin, Jeritza, Melchior, Melba, Patti, Pinza, Schipa, Caruso, Farrar, Steber, Gobbi, and many more—270 performers in all. Index. 199pp. 8⅜ x 11¼.   23575-0 Pa. $6.50

J. S. BACH, Albert Schweitzer. Great full-length study of Bach, life, background to music, music, by foremost modern scholar. Ernest Newman translation. 650 musical examples. Total of 928pp. 5⅜ x 8½. (Available in U.S. only)   21631-4, 21632-2 Pa., Two-vol. set $11.00

COMPLETE PIANO SONATAS, Ludwig van Beethoven. All sonatas in the fine Schenker edition, with fingering, analytical material. One of best modern editions. Total of 615pp. 9 x 12. (Available in U.S. only)
23134-8, 23135-6 Pa., Two-vol. set $15.00

KEYBOARD MUSIC, J. S. Bach. Bach-Gesellschaft edition. For harpsichord, piano, other keyboard instruments. English Suites, French Suites, Six Partitas, Goldberg Variations, Two-Part Inventions, Three-Part Sinfonias. 312pp. 8⅛ x 11. (Available in U.S. only)   22360-4 Pa. **$6.95**

FOUR SYMPHONIES IN FULL SCORE, Franz Schubert. Schubert's four most popular symphonies: No. 4 in C Minor ("Tragic"); No. 5 in B-flat Major; No. 8 in B Minor ("Unfinished"); No. 9 in C Major ("Great"). Breitkopf & Hartel edition. Study score. 261pp. 9⅜ x 12¼.
23681-1 Pa. $6.50

THE AUTHENTIC GILBERT & SULLIVAN SONGBOOK, W. S. Gilbert, A. S. Sullivan. Largest selection available; 92 songs, uncut, original keys, in piano rendering approved by Sullivan. Favorites and lesser-known fine numbers. Edited with plot synopses by James Spero. 3 illustrations. 399pp. 9 x 12.   23482-7 Pa. $9.95

PRINCIPLES OF ORCHESTRATION, Nikolay Rimsky-Korsakov. Great classical orchestrator provides fundamentals of tonal resonance, progression of parts, voice and orchestra, tutti effects, much else in major document. 330pp. of musical excerpts. 489pp. 6½ x 9¼. 21266-1 Pa. $7.50

TRISTAN UND ISOLDE, Richard Wagner. Full orchestral score with complete instrumentation. Do not confuse with piano reduction. Commentary by Felix Mottl, great Wagnerian conductor and scholar. Study score. 655pp. 8⅛ x 11. 22915-7 Pa. $13.95

REQUIEM IN FULL SCORE, Giuseppe Verdi. Immensely popular with choral groups and music lovers. Republication of edition published by C. F. Peters, Leipzig, n. d. German frontmaker in English translation. Glossary. Text in Latin. Study score. 204pp. 9⅜ x 12¼. 23682-X Pa. $6.00

COMPLETE CHAMBER MUSIC FOR STRINGS, Felix Mendelssohn. All of Mendelssohn's chamber music: Octet, 2 Quintets, 6 Quartets, and Four Pieces for String Quartet. (Nothing with piano is included). Complete works edition (1874-7). Study score. 283 pp. 9⅜ x 12¼. 23679-X Pa. $7.50

POPULAR SONGS OF NINETEENTH-CENTURY AMERICA, edited by Richard Jackson. 64 most important songs: "Old Oaken Bucket," "Arkansas Traveler," "Yellow Rose of Texas," etc. Authentic original sheet music, full introduction and commentaries. 290pp. 9 x 12. 23270-0 Pa. $7.95

COLLECTED PIANO WORKS, Scott Joplin. Edited by Vera Brodsky Lawrence. Practically all of Joplin's piano works—rags, two-steps, marches, waltzes, etc., 51 works in all. Extensive introduction by Rudi Blesh. Total of 345pp. 9 x 12. 23106-2 Pa. $14.95

BASIC PRINCIPLES OF CLASSICAL BALLET, Agrippina Vaganova. Great Russian theoretician, teacher explains methods for teaching classical ballet; incorporates best from French, Italian, Russian schools. 118 illustrations. 175pp. 5⅜ x 8½. 22036-2 Pa. $2.50

CHINESE CHARACTERS, L. Wieger. Rich analysis of 2300 characters according to traditional systems into primitives. Historical-semantic analysis to phonetics (Classical Mandarin) and radicals. 820pp. 6⅛ x 9¼. 21321-8 Pa. $10.00

EGYPTIAN LANGUAGE: EASY LESSONS IN EGYPTIAN HIERO-GLYPHICS, E. A. Wallis Budge. Foremost Egyptologist offers Egyptian grammar, explanation of hieroglyphics, many reading texts, dictionary of symbols. 246pp. 5 x 7½. (Available in U.S. only) 21394-3 Clothbd. $7.50

AN ETYMOLOGICAL DICTIONARY OF MODERN ENGLISH, Ernest Weekley. Richest, fullest work, by foremost British lexicographer. Detailed word histories. Inexhaustible. Do not confuse this with *Concise Etymological Dictionary*, which is abridged. Total of 856pp. 6½ x 9¼. 21873-2, 21874-0 Pa., Two-vol. set $12.00

CATALOGUE OF DOVER BOOKS

A MAYA GRAMMAR, Alfred M. Tozzer. Practical, useful English-language grammar by the Harvard anthropologist who was one of the three greatest American scholars in the area of Maya culture. Phonetics, grammatical processes, syntax, more. 301pp. 5⅜ x 8½. 23465-7 Pa. $4.00

THE JOURNAL OF HENRY D. THOREAU, edited by Bradford Torrey, F. H. Allen. Complete reprinting of 14 volumes, 1837-61, over two million words; the sourcebooks for *Walden,* etc. Definitive. All original sketches, plus 75 photographs. Introduction by Walter Harding. Total of 1804pp. 8½ x 12¼. 20312-3, 20313-1 Clothbd., Two-vol. set $50.00

CLASSIC GHOST STORIES, Charles Dickens and others. 18 wonderful stories you've wanted to reread: "The Monkey's Paw," "The House and the Brain," "The Upper Berth," "The Signalman," "Dracula's Guest," "The Tapestried Chamber," etc. Dickens, Scott, Mary Shelley, Stoker, etc. 330pp. 5⅜ x 8½. 20735-8 Pa. $4.50

SEVEN SCIENCE FICTION NOVELS, H. G. Wells. Full novels. *First Men in the Moon, Island of Dr. Moreau, War of the Worlds, Food of the Gods, Invisible Man, Time Machine, In the Days of the Comet.* A basic science-fiction library. 1015pp. 5⅜ x 8½. (Available in U.S. only)
20264-X Clothbd. $8.95

ARMADALE, Wilkie Collins. Third great mystery novel by the author of *The Woman in White* and *The Moonstone.* Ingeniously plotted narrative shows an exceptional command of character, incident and mood. Original magazine version with 40 illustrations. 597pp. 5⅜ x 8½.
23429-0 Pa. $6.00

MASTERS OF MYSTERY, H. Douglas Thomson. The first book in English (1931) devoted to history and aesthetics of detective story. Poe, Doyle, LeFanu, Dickens, many others, up to 1930. New introduction and notes by E. F. Bleiler. 288pp. 5⅜ x 8½. (Available in U.S. only)
23606-4 Pa. $4.00

FLATLAND, E. A. Abbott. Science-fiction classic explores life of 2-D being in 3-D world. Read also as introduction to thought about hyperspace. Introduction by Banesh Hoffmann. 16 illustrations. 103pp. 5⅜ x 8½.
20001-9 Pa. $2.00

THREE SUPERNATURAL NOVELS OF THE VICTORIAN PERIOD, edited, with an introduction, by E. F. Bleiler. Reprinted complete and unabridged, three great classics of the supernatural: *The Haunted Hotel* by Wilkie Collins, *The Haunted House at Latchford* by Mrs. J. H. Riddell, and *The Lost Stradivarious* by J. Meade Falkner. 325pp. 5⅜ x 8½.
22571-2 Pa. $4.00

AYESHA: THE RETURN OF "SHE," H. Rider Haggard. Virtuoso sequel featuring the great mythic creation, Ayesha, in an adventure that is fully as good as the first book, *She.* Original magazine version, with 47 original illustrations by Maurice Greiffenhagen. 189pp. 6½ x 9¼.
23649-8 Pa. $3.50

UNCLE SILAS, J. Sheridan LeFanu. Victorian Gothic mystery novel, considered by many best of period, even better than Collins or Dickens. Wonderful psychological terror. Introduction by Frederick Shroyer. 436pp. 5⅜ x 8½.						21715-9 Pa. $6.00

JURGEN, James Branch Cabell. The great erotic fantasy of the 1920's that delighted thousands, shocked thousands more. Full final text, Lane edition with 13 plates by Frank Pape. 346pp. 5⅜ x 8½.
						23507-6 Pa. $4.50

THE CLAVERINGS, Anthony Trollope. Major novel, chronicling aspects of British Victorian society, personalities. Reprint of Cornhill serialization, 16 plates by M. Edwards; first reprint of full text. Introduction by Norman Donaldson. 412pp. 5⅜ x 8½.			23464-9 Pa. $5.00

KEPT IN THE DARK, Anthony Trollope. Unusual short novel about Victorian morality and abnormal psychology by the great English author. Probably the first American publication. Frontispiece by Sir John Millais. 92pp. 6½ x 9¼.					23609-9 Pa. $2.50

RALPH THE HEIR, Anthony Trollope. Forgotten tale of illegitimacy, inheritance. Master novel of Trollope's later years. Victorian country estates, clubs, Parliament, fox hunting, world of fully realized characters. Reprint of 1871 edition. 12 illustrations by F. A. Faser. 434pp. of text. 5⅜ x 8½.					23642-0 Pa. $5.00

YEKL and THE IMPORTED BRIDEGROOM AND OTHER STORIES OF THE NEW YORK GHETTO, Abraham Cahan. Film *Hester Street* based on *Yekl* (1896). Novel, other stories among first about Jewish immigrants of N.Y.'s East Side. Highly praised by W. D. Howells—Cahan "a new star of realism." New introduction by Bernard G. Richards. 240pp. 5⅜ x 8½.					22427-9 Pa. $3.50

THE HIGH PLACE, James Branch Cabell. Great fantasy writer's enchanting comedy of disenchantment set in 18th-century France. Considered by some critics to be even better than his famous *Jurgen*. 10 illustrations and numerous vignettes by noted fantasy artist Frank C. Pape. 320pp. 5⅜ x 8½.					23670-6 Pa. $4.00

ALICE'S ADVENTURES UNDER GROUND, Lewis Carroll. Facsimile of ms. Carroll gave Alice Liddell in 1864. Different in many ways from final Alice. Handlettered, illustrated by Carroll. Introduction by Martin Gardner. 128pp. 5⅜ x 8½.				21482-6 Pa. $2.00

FAVORITE ANDREW LANG FAIRY TALE BOOKS IN MANY COLORS, Andrew Lang. The four Lang favorites in a boxed set—the complete *Red, Green, Yellow* and *Blue* Fairy Books. 164 stories; 439 illustrations by Lancelot Speed, Henry Ford and G. P. Jacomb Hood. Total of about 1500pp. 5⅜ x 8½.			23407-X Boxed set, Pa. $14.95

HOUSEHOLD STORIES BY THE BROTHERS GRIMM. All the great Grimm stories: "Rumpelstiltskin," "Snow White," "Hansel and Gretel," etc., with 114 illustrations by Walter Crane. 269pp. 5⅜ x 8½.
21080-4 Pa. $3.50

SLEEPING BEAUTY, illustrated by Arthur Rackham. Perhaps the fullest, most delightful version ever, told by C. S. Evans. Rackham's best work. 49 illustrations. 110pp. 7⅞ x 10¾. 22756-1 Pa. $2.50

AMERICAN FAIRY TALES, L. Frank Baum. Young cowboy lassoes Father Time; dummy in Mr. Floman's department store window comes to life; and 10 other fairy tales. 41 illustrations by N. P. Hall, Harry Kennedy, Ike Morgan, and Ralph Gardner. 209pp. 5⅜ x 8½. 23643-9 Pa. $3.00

THE WONDERFUL WIZARD OF OZ, L. Frank Baum. Facsimile in full color of America's finest children's classic. Introduction by Martin Gardner. 143 illustrations by W. W. Denslow. 267pp. 5⅜ x 8½.
20691-2 Pa. $3.50

THE TALE OF PETER RABBIT, Beatrix Potter. The inimitable Peter's terrifying adventure in Mr. McGregor's garden, with all 27 wonderful, full-color Potter illustrations. 55pp. 4¼ x 5½. (Available in U.S. only)
22827-4 Pa. $1.25

THE STORY OF KING ARTHUR AND HIS KNIGHTS, Howard Pyle. Finest children's version of life of King Arthur. 48 illustrations by Pyle. 131pp. 6⅛ x 9¼. 21445-1 Pa. $4.95

CARUSO'S CARICATURES, Enrico Caruso. Great tenor's remarkable caricatures of self, fellow musicians, composers, others. Toscanini, Puccini, Farrar, etc. Impish, cutting, insightful. 473 illustrations. Preface by M. Sisca. 217pp. 8⅜ x 11¼. 23528-9 Pa. $6.95

PERSONAL NARRATIVE OF A PILGRIMAGE TO ALMADINAH AND MECCAH, Richard Burton. Great travel classic by remarkably colorful personality. Burton, disguised as a Moroccan, visited sacred shrines of Islam, narrowly escaping death. Wonderful observations of Islamic life, customs, personalities. 47 illustrations. Total of 959pp. 5⅜ x 8½.
21217-3, 21218-1 Pa., Two-vol. set $12.00

INCIDENTS OF TRAVEL IN YUCATAN, John L. Stephens. Classic (1843) exploration of jungles of Yucatan, looking for evidences of Maya civilization. Travel adventures, Mexican and Indian culture, etc. Total of 669pp. 5⅜ x 8½. 20926-1, 20927-X Pa., Two-vol. set $7.90

AMERICAN LITERARY AUTOGRAPHS FROM WASHINGTON IRVING TO HENRY JAMES, Herbert Cahoon, et al. Letters, poems, manuscripts of Hawthorne, Thoreau, Twain, Alcott, Whitman, 67 other prominent American authors. Reproductions, full transcripts and commentary. Plus checklist of all American Literary Autographs in The Pierpont Morgan Library. Printed on exceptionally high-quality paper. 136 illustrations. 212pp. 9⅛ x 12¼. 23548-3 Pa. $12.50

CATALOGUE OF DOVER BOOKS

AN AUTOBIOGRAPHY, Margaret Sanger. Exciting personal account of hard-fought battle for woman's right to birth control, against prejudice, church, law. Foremost feminist document. 504pp. 5⅜ x 8½.
20470-7 Pa. $5.50

MY BONDAGE AND MY FREEDOM, Frederick Douglass. Born as a slave, Douglass became outspoken force in antislavery movement. The best of Douglass's autobiographies. Graphic description of slave life. Introduction by P. Foner. 464pp. 5⅜ x 8½. 22457-0 Pa. $5.50

LIVING MY LIFE, Emma Goldman. Candid, no holds barred account by foremost American anarchist: her own life, anarchist movement, famous contemporaries, ideas and their impact. Struggles and confrontations in America, plus deportation to U.S.S.R. Shocking inside account of persecution of anarchists under Lenin. 13 plates. Total of 944pp. 5⅜ x 8½.
22543-7, 22544-5 Pa., Two-vol. set $12.00

LETTERS AND NOTES ON THE MANNERS, CUSTOMS AND CONDITIONS OF THE NORTH AMERICAN INDIANS, George Catlin. Classic account of life among Plains Indians: ceremonies, hunt, warfare, etc. Dover edition reproduces for first time all original paintings. 312 plates. 572pp. of text. 6⅛ x 9¼. 22118-0, 22119-9 Pa.. Two-vol. set $12.00

THE MAYA AND THEIR NEIGHBORS, edited by Clarence L. Hay, others. Synoptic view of Maya civilization in broadest sense, together with Northern, Southern neighbors. Integrates much background, valuable detail not elsewhere. Prepared by greatest scholars: Kroeber, Morley, Thompson, Spinden, Vaillant, many others. Sometimes called Tozzer Memorial Volume. 60 illustrations, linguistic map. 634pp. 5⅜ x 8½.
23510-6 Pa. $7.50

HANDBOOK OF THE INDIANS OF CALIFORNIA, A. L. Kroeber. Foremost American anthropologist offers complete ethnographic study of each group. Monumental classic. 459 illustrations, maps. 995pp. 5⅜ x 8½.
23368-5 Pa. $13.00

SHAKTI AND SHAKTA, Arthur Avalon. First book to give clear, cohesive analysis of Shakta doctrine, Shakta ritual and Kundalini Shakti (yoga). Important work by one of world's foremost students of Shaktic and Tantric thought. 732pp. 5⅜ x 8½. (Available in U.S. only)
23645-5 Pa. $7.95

AN INTRODUCTION TO THE STUDY OF THE MAYA HIEROGLYPHS, Syvanus Griswold Morley. Classic study by one of the truly great figures in hieroglyph research. Still the best introduction for the student for reading Maya hieroglyphs. New introduction by J. Eric S. Thompson. 117 illustrations. 284pp. 5⅜ x 8½. 23108-9 Pa. $4.00

A STUDY OF MAYA ART, Herbert J. Spinden. Landmark classic interprets Maya symbolism, estimates styles, covers ceramics, architecture, murals, stone carvings as artforms. Still a basic book in area. New introduction by J. Eric Thompson. Over 750 illustrations. 341pp. 8⅜ x 11¼.
21235-1 Pa. $6.95

GEOMETRY, RELATIVITY AND THE FOURTH DIMENSION, Rudolf Rucker. Exposition of fourth dimension, means of visualization, concepts of relativity as Flatland characters continue adventures. Popular, easily followed yet accurate, profound. 141 illustrations. 133pp. 5⅜ x 8½.
23400-2 Pa. $2.75

THE ORIGIN OF LIFE, A. I. Oparin. Modern classic in biochemistry, the first rigorous examination of possible evolution of life from nitrocarbon compounds. Non-technical, easily followed. Total of 295pp. 5⅜ x 8½.
60213-3 Pa. $4.00

PLANETS, STARS AND GALAXIES, A. E. Fanning. Comprehensive introductory survey: the sun, solar system, stars, galaxies, universe, cosmology; quasars, radio stars, etc. 24pp. of photographs. 189pp. 5⅜ x 8½. (Available in U.S. only)
21680-2 Pa. $3.75

THE THIRTEEN BOOKS OF EUCLID'S ELEMENTS, translated with introduction and commentary by Sir Thomas L. Heath. Definitive edition. Textual and linguistic notes, mathematical analysis, 2500 years of critical commentary. Do not confuse with abridged school editions. Total of 1414pp. 5⅜ x 8½.   60088-2, 60089-0, 60090-4 Pa., Three-vol. set $18.50

Prices subject to change without notice.

Available at your book dealer or write for free catalogue to Dept. GI, Dover Publications, Inc., 180 Varick St., N.Y., N.Y. 10014. Dover publishes more than 175 books each year on science, elementary and advanced mathematics, biology, music, art, literary history, social sciences and other areas.